A Mother's Manual for Self Care:

An A-Z Pocket Manual Supporting Moms Through Unexpected, Common Emotions

Written By, Michelle Schrag

Manuscript Consultant, Terry Pfister

© 2015 Michelle Schrag

D1374260

A Mother's Manual for Self-Love

TABLE OF CONTENTS

5. Introduction

6. Anger: I Give Myself the Love I Need

10. Control: I Let Go and Allow

15. Defensive: I am Safe and at Peace with My Choices

18. Desperation: I am Enough

22. Embarrassment: I Accept My Child as She is

26. Fear: I Replace Fear with Trust That Life is For Me

28. Feeling like a Victim: I Create My Life

32. Gossip: I Release Unhealthy Judgment to Find Joy

37. Guilt: I Let Go and Let Life Happen

41. Helplessness: I am Present

44. I am Not My Mother: I Accept and Forgive

49. It's Just the Way it is: I Choose My Unique Experience

54. Jealousy: I'm Happy for Her and I'm Open to the Same Thing Happening To Me

57. Judgment: I Choose Compassion

63. Living in the Past or Future: I Live in the Now

67. Making Comparisons: I Honor My Child

72. My Hands are Tied: I am a Healer

76. People-Pleasing: I Give and Receive in Perfect Balance

80. Playing Roles: I Express Myself as Authentically Me

84. Resentment: I Walk in My Own Power

88. Resistance: I Surrender to Allowing

92. Self-Deprecation: I Accept and Appreciate Myself

96. Shame: I Come from Unconditional Love

100. Things will Never Change: I Know that a New Moment is Always Coming

104. Unhealthy Boundaries: I See Myself as Valuable

108. Worry: I Trust in the Flow

LESSONS TO SUPPORT YOU

113. Finding Peace through Forgiveness

120. Releasing a Burden

122. Conversation with Your Future Self

124. Conversation with Your Grown-up Child

126. Start a Worry Journal

129. Beginning the Day Meditation

131. Ending the Day Meditation

132. Preparing for a Family Change

135. Mother's Self-Love Meditation

137. Connecting with Your Inner Child Meditation

139. While You Work Meditation

141. Unconditional Love Meditation

143. Changing Your Behavior

144. Affirmations

145. Positive nightly "prayer"

146. Thank you Page

Introduction

When I started this process, it was for me. I found so many parenting books! In fact I probably had, at one point, an entire bookshelf of them. What I needed though was help with *me*. If I didn't trust myself, or feel confident in what I was doing, how could I follow through with a parenting style? So I started writing down my uncomfortable emotions, looking for the triggers, and then using my spiritual counseling class knowledge and life experience to find the root and then figure out ways to help me get through them. I was tired of feeling regretful, clueless, like I was always just reacting to parenting situations, rather than being purposeful with them. After a while I had so much information and it was really helpful to me, so I thought I should share it. Every single word was written in the moment, of a situation or an emotion whether it was my moment or a friend's moment.

This book is a safe space to be honest with yourself. A lot that comes up for us moms are things that we may not necessarily know how to talk with someone else about. Here, you can open up to whatever emotion you are having and get the healthy supportive words that you need. The exercises in the back of the book are there to help you build a strong anchor for yourself so you can then parent the way you want to.

I don't mean to exclude dads. This book is for *parents*. Because I'm a mom, I don't feel qualified to write for a dad. Although I do know that we all experience the same emotions as parents. So please, don't take offense if you are a dad. I hope that you find comfort in these words as well.

I have a passion for helping moms (parents) to learn to love and accept themselves. My hope is that this book is a back pocket tool that gets used and passed on and shared so that we can all be kinder to ourselves and each other.

Anger: I Give Myself the Love I Need

My first real experience with out of control anger was when I was in college. I was dating a guy in what was a seriously co-dependent relationship, complete with cheating, fighting, and jealousy – everything that you can imagine in a very unbalanced, young relationship. I remember the phone conversation with him when I found out he'd cheated on me. I was furious, and he kept hanging up on me! I thought my head was going to explode. My anger felt horrible and embarrassingly desperate.

As I grew older, healing and maturing and learning self love, I really didn't experience much anger. Then, my children came along, and I was dealing with lack of sleep and the teasing and fighting between them. Anger started trickling my way again.

Anger is an emotion that has been difficult for me, especially when it comes to expressing it in a healthy way. There always seems to be a flood of guilt afterwards. I never learned how to express anger in a healthy way. My parents never fought in front of me and my siblings. Then there was that awful experience in college, which I thought I'd healed. My anger has been full of shame because I've judged it as something wrong and unnecessary, and bad like "I'm a bad person because I'm angry." I even thought for awhile, "I'm too *evolved* to feel angry, so what am I missing?"

When I'm *reacting* in anger, there's a false belief that says my anger is keeping me in control. After responding in anger when my kids are fighting, I've thought to myself, "I know this isn't working, but I don't know what else to do!" That's my signal that I'm in the false belief that anger is the only way to respond. When I am feeling angry, it's time to stop and see what it is the anger is trying to show me. Am I tired or frustrated? Am I doing too many things at once? Do I feel unappreciated, disrespected or taken advantage of? What is *causing* this anger?

A book on anger by Buddhist teacher, Thich Nhat Hanh, entered my life at just the right time. He describes anger as being part of the human experience, and he compares its presence to how we experience the organs in our body. If you have a stomachache, for example, you might rest or take some medicine, but you *want* your stomach to feel better. If you have a headache, you might choose to sleep or take an aspirin – whatever will make your head feel better. Our anger is like an organ in our body. When it is not acting up, your "anger-organ" is quiet and totally invisible. When anger flares up, your "anger-organ" needs healing too. That healing means *loving* attention – not shame, defensiveness or resentment. Our "anger-organ" needs to be calmed and fed with love so that it can transform back into it's quiet intuitive self.

Use your anger to reveal how you need to love yourself.

That beautiful way of looking at anger removes any judgment in me, and creates a peaceful space inside that rests between my calm, wise "inner being" and the anger itself. That space allows me to breathe. And since my anger is a signal in my body that something is off, it can't be ignored or pushed down. It must be looked at. My anger is telling me I'm feeling off and I need to give myself some attention to see what it is.

When we judge our anger as "bad", we separate out a piece of who we are. You might say to yourself that your anger is a bad thing so part of you is a bad thing. And, when we call parts of ourselves "bad", we start to spiral down into self-loathing. We'll continually separate and compartmentalize these bad parts of ourselves - but they'll remain a part of our lives. Then, when we parent from feeling like we are bad, we will continue to unconsciously find ways to prove that we are bad, by losing it, being angry. We also will start judging parts of our children as bad.

I believe that what I focus on is what I experience in my life. My life is a reflection of my thoughts. That means that what I am feeling inside has a direct effect on how I perceive my daily life. If I'm feeling more anger than I usually do, what inside of me is looking for a voice? What needs to be heard? When I can use anger for its purpose, to alarm me that I am in need of something, than I feel grateful for it.

As human beings, we are all going to have feelings, and we can learn so much from them. It's like the bathtub in your home. When you need it, you turn on the faucet, plug and fill the tub, and climb in. When you're done, you unplug the drain and get out. You don't even think about the bathtub during the day. You just *know* it's there. But, what if you left the faucet running all day with the drain plugged? Your bathroom would flood, if not most of the rooms nearby. This is a metaphor for letting your anger run your life. When you have an obtrusive emotion like anger happening in your life, and you are pushing it down, trying to ignore it, judging it as bad, it runs until it overflows, and then your home (your body) is affected. Use your feelings when you need them, and then, just let them be.

You are a good person - totally and completely. Your anger does not define who you are. Love yourself through it! Watch how it flares up and listen to what it is telling you. I think you will find that there is always a message. And maybe the message is simple: you need sleep. You need self-care. You need love. Use it for what it is there for. Do not judge yourself as bad for reacting to your anger. Your anger wants to be quiet too, so let it come and go without judgment.

Affirmations to Change Anger into Love

When I change my thinking, I change my life.

Anger is an organ in my body. I love and nurture myself when anger acts up.

I remove any and all judgment of my anger. I allow anger to be just what it is – a signal that something is off in my life.

I am more than any anger that I might feel. I choose to accept that truth whenever anger starts acting up.

A Mother's Manual for Self-Love

I am made of unconditional love. Anger is a human experience that deserves loving attention.

Control: I Let Go and Allow

Control is a big issue for many of us moms, and the subject could probably fill its own book! You have mouths to feed, their homework to get done, a house to maintain, and usually multiple schedules to keep. You also watch the news and you might feel scared to trust life after hearing about these terrible things that happen each day.

This chapter is not talking about the normal daily controls that need to be in place for our families to function. The kind of control I'm talking about is the one that you feel chained to. The control that feels like if you don't have it your world will crumble. It's something that is *not* helpful or healthy for you or your children. This "control" comes from fear – like feeling that I need to take over my child's actions so that he or she does what *I* would do and so she/he is safe. It's a control that says, "It must go my way or I am a failure." It can feel panicky, anxiety filled and all consuming.

When I am in the place of needing to over- control, I am in a false belief that I am only safe when people, places and things are right where I want them to be. I am thinking that if things *don't* go my way - if my child doesn't listen to me, if the house isn't perfect, if my schedule isn't on time, if I'm not there - than my whole world will crumble and people will judge me. It's a fear that, when I am not in control, I'm scared, I am not worthy, valuable, or not being respected.

Trust that what's happening right now is meant to be.

How do you move away from this fear of losing control towards *allowing* for more healthy control and more trust and peace in your life? When things aren't perfect, or going the way we wanted them to we feel like our world will crumble. The truth is that the love between you and your family is being energized and strengthened even when things aren't perfect. Learning to let go and allow for things to unfold is healthy for you and for your family. It shows your children that you trust life. What a great example!

10

Control because I don't trust the world

The news is scary sometimes. Maybe you don't trust
life! There is so much bad news that we hear, and we
hear about illnesses, and shootings, and abuse. It's
scary to send a child into the world when we are
inundated by all of this bad news. I might want to strictly
structure my child's day so that he is safe all of the time.
I might be extremely specific about what my child eats to
keep him healthy. I might be a "helicopter parent" that is
in every moment of my child's day, controlling every
second. When this becomes all consuming, that's when
we need to take a step back and find a way to trust the
world around us so that we can enjoy life. It might take
baby steps, and that is okay.

I was talking with a man in his 60s who told me that he
spent years and years worrying about and controlling
everything in his life. And none of the things that he
obsessed about ever came true. He wished so much
that he could go back and change all of that wasted
energy and anxiety. He wished he could go back and
enjoy life. I want you to honor him by doing this *now*.
Not when it's too late and you are filled with regret.

Turn the news off. You can read about what's important
online. If you have friends that like to talk about the bad
news in the world, and it triggers you to feel unhealthily
controlling of your family, try changing the subject with
those friends. You could even say, "I'm trying so hard
not to focus on these terrifying news stories - it scares
me too much! Could we maybe spend some time talking
about some of the good things going on around us?"

Remind yourself that your kids will learn independence
and trust by their experiences. Give them some wiggle
room and see how you feel about it. Then, you can give
them a little more. Be kind to yourself through the
process knowing that you are slowly teaching them how
to trust themselves in a healthy way.

Over- Control because I feel safe when all is in order and I'm on time

One thing to affirm is "Right now, I am ok" "But what about running late for gymnastics? I hate being late!" "You are still okay" "But what about the disaster in my kitchen?" "You are still okay" "I didn't get to wash my face last night, and I'm not sure the kids got any vegetables yesterday, and I didn't get my child signed up for that math class that everybody else's kids are doing!" "You are still okay." You are truly okay, with no strings attached. When you and I *know* this, we find ourselves coming at challenges from a different place. No matter what is taking place in your life, you can know and trust that what is happening is exactly what is supposed to be happening.

Start seeing the perceived disorder as ok. I remind myself that keeping a house perfect with children in it is, well, nearly impossible! If I'm stressed out thinking that I am not a good mom because my house is not in order, that's an unnecessary and inaccurate judgment I'm making, right? And that judgment isn't supportive to me, or to anyone around me. A clean house with a stressed-out mom is not worth it!

Sure, I know many of us might feel safer and more secure when we have everything in order. We might even use the state of our surroundings to get that peace we can't find in our minds. And it *does* feel good to have a clean house! Controlling our surroundings creates a space of temporary peace and harmony. But wouldn't it be nice to feel safety and order and harmony even when things in our homes are not perfect?

How do we find peace in the chaos? We change our perception. I was chatting with another mom recently about her home. She was telling me that she doesn't focus on cleaning the house. She said since she only has a few more years until her kids leave home to go to college, she wants to spend time with them! In a few years, after they leave the nest, she'll have a clean house. I still hold on to that new idea.

A Mother's Manual for Self-Love

Also - most of the time, when I feel like I need to control everything around me, I'm really scared about *something* in my life. If I work at figuring out what that *something* is, I can change it. Maybe I don't think there is enough time, or that if I'm not paying attention, something will happen to my child. Maybe I have a misperception that when my kids act out, or when things aren't perfect it is a direct reflection of me so I will domineer until I get what I want. It could be that I'm concerned about my child. Whatever fear is causing you to feel, see if you can let it go for a day. Allow for an imperfect house and instead do something with your child. You will feel so good! If you are running late, let yourself enjoy the drive to wherever you are going. Know that there is perfect timing in life. Allow for you and your children to make mistakes. We're all perfect in our imperfections.

We might forget sometimes that we're safe when things don't go the way we want them to go. That's okay. Everything is okay as it is. You and I can let go. The world will not crumble around us if our plan of control does not happen the way we wanted it to. Although the voice in your head might tell you otherwise, when you release the fear and the need to control your world, you find out that everything is the way it's supposed to be. And that's real peace.

Affirmations for Letting Go and Allowing

My kids' normal growth patterns will include choices that they make that I don't like. That is *ok*. I allow for my kids to learn natural consequences and I love them through it.

I accept my kids for how they are, knowing even when growing up doesn't look pretty everything is happening for their growth.

When things don't go the way I want them to go, I am safe.

Today I look for the good news in life.

I let go! I let go! I let go!

Today, I let go and trust in life.

I am safe all of the time. I let go of my false controls and let my true nature shine through.

I accept everything in my life today – the imperfections and the perfections. It is all good.

I let myself breathe. I let my anxiety calm. I allow for my life to be lived as it is.

In the midst of the chaos, I find my deep inner peace and let go.

Defensive: I am safe and at peace with my choices

There is a time and a place to defend a child, a belief system, a law, a social issue, a political view. This is normal and appropriate. When I talk about being "defensive" here, I'm talking about that hyper-trigger that we get when we feel attacked and then we react in a way that we regret later. I'm talking about that unhealthy reaction that keeps us thinking small, as if we are at war and someone has to win and it will be me. I'm not talking about healthy debate and appropriate defense.

There is room for every single one of us to be who we are. There is no need for anyone to try and change you or call you "wrong" or "bad" when you do something different from the way they would. When someone does that, they are doing it out of fear and they are probably doing it out of love. Because it works for them, and it makes them happy to think that it will work for you too. Feeling attacked and then responding by being defensive when someone makes an opinion or judgment about you or someone you love is so common. It's a protective measure.

If I'm not at war, there is nothing to defend.

Please consider this. Your life doesn't need defending. Your decisions don't need defending. You can make your choices for yourself and your family as you see fit. You are more than capable at deciding what is best for your life. If you feel attacked by someone's judgments, tone of their voice, or beliefs, *remind yourself that their judgment/tone of voice/beliefs have nothing to do with you.* "You don't have to understand my choices because they are mine. I am happy that you have found what works best for you."

As parents, we have so many different choices to make for our kids. It starts with breastfeeding or not, to public or private school, to when to let your child get a cell phone, to video games, what to believe in, how to believe, what to feed our kids, etc. That is just a few of many. I had a woman tell me, after I told her where I lived, that she would never live in my neighborhood, and then she gave me several (very judgmental) reasons why not and then she shared about her brand new huge home closer to downtown. What I realized is that if someone has an issue with a choice that I made, it's in *his or her* head - not mine, It is on *his or her* mind, not mine, unless I let it get under my skin. I'm in a place now where I feel compassion for someone who looks down on me for a choice I made because that is a lot of fear to live with. I don't need to defend my choice. I can listen with compassion and I can continue with the choice that I made.

When people share things that they say are the "only way" to think or believe, I feel defensive. We will run into all kinds of people when we move through this life, and learning to let people be, and not take what they say personally, is such a huge leap towards unconditional acceptance. The people I've always found I like to learn from are the ones who are quietly doing their thing, without so much noise, leading by example. The kind of person who you might say, "Wow, she is so positive all the time - I wonder what she does to be that inspiring?"

I've practiced laughing when I feel that defensiveness pop up. I've practiced listening from an unconditional place so that it doesn't get under my skin. I've practiced letting it go, I've practiced not taking things personally, so I don't play wishful conversations over and over in my head. I've visualized removing any buttons ("she knows how to push my buttons!"). Most importantly, I've practiced unconditional acceptance - knowing, first, anytime, no matter what it looks like, any time someone tries to put his or her life choices onto you, they are afraid. No one knows what goes on behind someone's door. We all have our reasons for being who we are.

It's ironic, but our biggest angels are those that we have the hardest time with. How can I learn to be a better person if I don't have someone challenging me every step of the way? Look at those who stretch you as someone giving you the opportunity to practice unconditional acceptance. Put down your weapons. You have nothing to defend. You are good just as you are. And so are they.

Affirmations for: I am safe and at peace with my choices.

I am at peace with all of my choices in life.

I lay down my weapons and I show up in peace.

I am confident in who I am and the choices I make all of the time.

I let people be where they are with no judgment of where that is.

I create healthy boundaries for my family and myself.

There is room for everyone to be who he or she authentically is.

Desperation: I am Enough

My daughter Sophie was born five weeks early and she stayed in the hospital for 8 days, Three days after her birth my son came down with a stomach flu. I wanted to visit Sophie, *and* to be with Cooper. I would pump Sophie's milk before visiting her in the neo natal intensive care unit every day, and at home I was cleaning up after my sick, little boy. By day five, both my husband and I came down with flu. There I was, pumping milk for my daughter while lying on the kitchen floor with a bucket next to me. Of course, I had just given birth, so my body was in the midst of healing as well. I felt truly desperate! How was I supposed to bring a preemie baby into a home filled with stomach flu?

More recently - following the deep, internal work I've been doing to create a life of unconditional love and acceptance - I awakened one morning and just *knew,* before I even got out of bed, that my day was going to be off. Desperation started welling up. All the kids were sick and up all night and I was a mess. At one point during the day, I hid in the bathroom, praying desperately for a change over and over and screaming with all of my might - a silent scream that just poured out of me. I felt no love, no light, and no inner guidance.

All day long I'd kept saying to myself, "Michelle, use your techniques to get out of this." So I was honest with the kids about how I was feeling. I even asked out loud if there is such a thing as divine feminine energy to work through me. I breathed in peace- at least I tried - and meditated. I did just about everything I knew to do on a day like this. All of this worked a few times, for a moment. But again, it was short lived. Then I wrote an e-mail to some trusted friends, and described my day and how desperate I felt. This act of reaching out kept me from losing it. I learned in that moment that I'm human, and sometimes a human being just needs to be where she is. And that is perfect, just as it is.

Desperation usually means we are at our wits end. Whether its because of exhaustion, finances, illness, you name it - when we are overloaded we feel desperate. We could be going through much more in our life that we hadn't planned on. It can also mean we have said 'yes' to something that is not an authentic 'yes'. I know that, when I've felt desperate, I've usually forgotten that I am human, and that it's okay to have an *off* day or week or month. There's a false belief that tells me that I need to be perfect, and that it's not okay for me to feel so lost and depleted.

Let's use this feeling of desperation as a signal that something is out of balance (mentally, emotionally, or socially) inside our relationships or inside our life. We, as mothers, often tend to do *everything* because we feel like that is our responsibility. Whether you work out of the home or in it - we tend to take on more responsibilities than we need to. It feels like everyone needs us for something. Do you know who needs you the very most? You do. You need to be tended to before you can be there for everyone else.

Let go of desperate feelings by recognizing you are enough, just the way you are.

How do you let go? How can you do anything for yourself when you are feeling pulled in so many directions doing everything for everyone else? The first step is to check in with yourself. Do you have good boundaries around your relationships and/or your work? Maybe you are saying yes to more responsibilities than are healthy for you. Ask yourself questions like, "Does watching the neighbor's kids again feel like something I really want to do?" Or, "Does it feel good to be taking my child to this class on Tuesday nights, or do I feel like I'm saying 'yes' because of other reasons?" What you are looking for are your *internal* signals. Your body and your inner voice tell you what is good for you - or not so good for you. Listen to them!

Second, ask for help. Sometimes it feels like there is nothing we can change. Our lives are fuller than we can manage and there isn't anything we can do right now.

A Mother's Manual for Self-Love

When I described having the stomach flu earlier, I had my parents here, helping me and supporting me and the family. The day I woke up on the wrong side of the bed, I checked in with friends to remind myself that I wasn't alone. Asking for help can feel impossible. We don't want to be a burden on anyone else. Maybe we don't want to admit to our imperfection. But think about it: this is what friends are for. Friends are in our lives to support every aspect of us and we are there to support them. Please - reach out to someone if you are feeling desperate. You are not alone.

Another important practice when desperation hits is to be present. When I'm feeling desperate, it's usually because I'm feeling overwhelmed by my thoughts... maybe something from the past, or by what might come later. But if I truly allow myself to be in the now moment, (aware of what I can see, touch, hear), I find that there's nothing to feel desperate about. The desperation might actually be a story I've made up about something happening later – that hasn't happened.

When I was having that horrible day, I practiced being present with gusto. The dialogue in my head went, "I am walking up the stairs – the carpet is tan – Violet is in front of me - there is a picture on the wall..." Can you understand how there could be nothing left for me to stress over when I literally looked and described what was right in front of me? My mind couldn't make up stories about how the kids kept me up all night or how one of them is totally acting up so I am entitled to feel bad, or thinking of my schedule and letting it paralyze me. By staying in the now moment, I wasn't making myself feel worse by rehashing my "story".

When I remember and affirm the fact that *I am enough*, that I have enough, and that I am not alone, a small spark lights up inside of me. I feel a little more alive and that gets me through until bedtime. What I like to remember is that there is a sacredness to our motherhood, and it is supported by a deeper, larger feminine energy that is feeding us at all times, my simple awareness of it allows me to sense it and use it to support me. For example, calculus exists in the world, but unless I'm taking classes about it, I won't know anything about it. If I study and practice calculus, I will learn it. If I practice listening to that deeper intuitive voice, I will hear it more and more easily.

Know that what you need is inside of you, at all times – like energy, flow and peace - and it's ready for the taking. Give yourself the gift of allowing yourself to be where you need to be, whatever that looks like. You are a mother, so you are sourced right here and now with all of the knowledge that you need. You are always enough!

Affirmations for Declaring that You are Enough

There is always enough energy flowing everywhere around me.

I love myself right where I am, whatever it looks like.

I surrender into self -love.

I AM enough.

The energy, peace, the flow that I need is all inside of me. I activate it now.

My inner guidance helps me establish my day so that it is healthy for me and everyone involved.

I allow myself to be where I am, whatever that looks like.

I love myself however I show up. I am gentle with myself and with what I have to offer.

Embarrassment: I Accept My Child as She is

Have you ever been embarrassed by something your child has done? My daughter had a play date a few years back, and she was so excited for her friend to get here. When her friend arrived, my daughter immediately started complaining. She didn't want to share her toys, and was saying not-so-nice things to the friend like, "I don't want to play with you" and "I don't like you". This continued as, thankfully, her friend ignored my daughter's comments. My daughter and this girl have played together often so, needless to say, this situation was quite unexpected.

I tried talking with my daughter about how she was acting while in front of the other child's mom, only to have her start talking back to me. I felt like I was on stage and the other mom waited to see what I would say. Feeling pressured to parent the right way, I wanted to give her a consequence without shaming her. It was important to me to say the "right thing" so that the other mom would realize that I was aware of my daughter's behavior and that I was being fair. In my embarrassment, I took my daughter aside and asked her to have some alone-time until she felt ready to be a good friend. Her initial reaction was a tantrum but, in the end, we got through it. All the while I reminded myself that she is still learning how to *be* a friend.

Children go through phases. But, even knowing our kids behaviors can feel embarrassing! I started judging myself and whether or not I'm a good parent I also wondered if her friend's mother was judging me or my daughter. After some reflection, I realized that a false belief had shown its face, a false belief that says that everything my child does and says is defining who she is as a person – and me as a mother. And that is simply not true!

When we were living in Chicago my son said something in a group of boys thinking he would get a laugh and another parent said, "That wasn't a nice thing to say." I felt flooded with embarrassment, thinking, "Do these other parents think I'm not a good mother because my child said this? Do they think we talk like this in our house?"

Accept your child exactly where she is in her personal growth.

Here's what we moms need to remember in these situations. First, they are a perfect teaching opportunity for practicing non-judgment. We get to send love to ourselves and to our children, and to the other kids and parents who are involved. We get to *practice*. Kids learn through sharing, friendship, conversations, mood swings, connecting, and learning how to get a laugh. What a mom might judge as "not being nice" is a phase a child needs to go through in order to move to his next level of relationship and connection with others. We need to trust that our kids' paths are just that- *their* paths. Some kids will have easier paths than others. And what I know for sure is that the more we can collectively see kids as raw and vulnerable and testing behaviors along the way- instead of judging them will result in them feeling safer as they grow.

Second, when I judge my children or their actions as wrong, I set them up to feel shame, when they are just children learning their boundaries. We do not need to take it personally or we'll tend to parent out of embarrassment. Today I'm challenging myself to parent out of total balance between my heart and my head, as if my child and I are the only two people in the room. I don't need to impress anyone with what I'm saying to my child. I am still my child's number one fan, no matter what his behavior looks like. I also do my best to remember that my child is not me, living my childhood.... She will not have the same experience that I did.

Does that mean she doesn't face consequences for behaviors that hurt or disrespect herself or other people? No. And I work very hard (with mistakes a plenty!) at disciplining from love, not from embarrassment. And I need this reminder for new situations, as I feel much better when I am hearing and seeing my child from the perspective of unformed clay – not brokenness.

When I feel embarrassed about how my child has acted, I also believe that there is some insecurity there about my parenting. For all of us, this can be something to really dive into. In the story about my daughter and her play date pal, my first fear was that I hadn't raised my daughter to be a good friend. When my son said that disrespectful word, I feared that I hadn't raised my son to be considerate. Then I realized the truth. This situation is exactly how she is learning what it takes to be a good friend. That situation is exactly how he is learning his boundaries. The way I react or don't react to my children's words and actions is how they learn these lessons. And finally, the way I model my life is ultimately what will shine through.

When I'm with my child and start to sense a feeling of embarrassment for something that she is doing, I work to see - in that very moment - this experience as a teaching tool, and nothing more. I remind myself that she is still learning and that this doesn't define who she is. When I feel confident in my skin, I can then parent from a healthy place.

My mom tells a story about the first time she brought my brother to a play date and another child hit him. Feeling mortified, she thought, "My child will never do that!" A year later, it was my brother doing the same thing to another child. The more we accept other parents for *how* they parent, the less embarrassment we will feel when it's our child acting out.

Be proud of who your child is, knowing that you are guiding his journey and teaching him respect and boundaries. A competitive streak or willful behavior could very well be what takes your child to happiness someday. We can't interrupt their growth pattern, no matter how uncomfortable it is for us! That experience of my daughter acting so sassy with her friend was just a building block for her future. We are all in this together, Moms. Let's lighten our load by supporting each other with acceptance.

Affirmations for Accepting My Child as She Is

I accept my child and the way she chooses to show her emotions. It's authentic to her. I may not like it all of the time – and I still need to accept it.

When I feel a button is about to be pushed, I immediately become light as air so there is no button to push.

If I feel embarrassment coming on, I remind myself that my child is a beautiful work in progress.

I am armed with the perfect consequences for my child, whatever it is she is doing.

My child is on his perfect path all of the time, whatever it looks like.

I look at issues with my child as teaching situations. I get to teach my child the loving way to be.

I remove myself and my defenses when my child is acting out.

When my child says something that is disrespectful, I need to remember this as a teaching tool for showing boundaries - not an attacking moment of feeling embarrassed.

When my child is acting out, I remember that I am the caregiver responding with consequences, not the judge and jury.

I look to intuition and guidance for any issue that I need to pay closer attention to.

I am the perfect parent for my child.

Fear: I Move From a Place of Trust

Fear can run our lives. We are afraid to try something new. We are afraid to say "yes", we are afraid to say "no". We are afraid to change, we might feel afraid of different social settings. We feel scared when we listen to the news or we hear about certain illnesses, or accidents. We lash out at someone who thinks differently from us because we are afraid that our beliefs are being shot at. We make decisions based on our fear. Fears can be healthy - when they keep us from doing something dangerous that isn't good for us. And, fears can be all consuming and paralyzing keeping us from living in joy.

I think something that happens when we start feeling afraid is we start convincing ourselves that the fear is keeping us safe. Maybe we think it's inner guidance. "If I do x, y and z - I will feel safe." "If I stay away from x, y and z then I am safe." We are also coming from a place of complete mistrust. We feel like the weight of the world is on our shoulders and there is nothing to grab onto to help - but fear. We don't trust life itself.

Obsessive fear is never intuition. Intuition is the ability of knowing what you need to know right when you need to know it. Obsessive fear is a thought pattern that gets very comfortable in your head very quickly. It feels out of control and desperate. It can feel like a brick wall. No matter how big that brick wall feels, it's not real - it's imagination.

If you could play your thoughts out on a television screen, what would the show be about? What are your thoughts made up of? I think some of us might have a good old-fashioned horror movie if our thoughts were put on the big screen. And how many of those fearful thoughts have actually come true in your life? Usually the answer is none.

If fear is running my life, I am desperately afraid of being vulnerable and hurt. I am completely untrusting of life. And so many of us have been through some really awful experiences - it's no wonder we feel afraid. Learning to

26

over come that fear though, will help you live a more fulfilling life. Would you consider taking a baby step like, "I'm going to say 'yes' to that social outing that I normally would have said 'no' to". "I'm going to let the house have a little mess in it trusting that I'll be ok even when things aren't perfect." "I'm going to trust that I'm safe at night and let myself have a good night of sleep." Say, "yes" to something that scares you. (Within reason of course!)

When I feel fearful, the quickest way for me to get out of it is to ask a few simple questions of myself. "What can I see right now?" "What can I feel?" "What can I hear?" These questions catapult me out of my fears and bring me into the moment. When I'm being present, I can't be afraid. If something scary is about to happen, like a shot, or a surgery, or a presentation - I can't be afraid if I am actively pursuing the present moment. I have used this so many times in my life and it works every single time. You can't be in fear and be present at the same time.

You are bigger than your fear - no matter how consuming it feels. Replace your fear with faith. Make room for intuition to guide you. And let joy back into your life.

Affirmations for Moving From a Place of Trust

I replace my fear with faith

I let go of my fears and I relax into trusting that all is well

I let go of this thought pattern that fear is a healthy guide

I embrace life knowing it is FOR me and I trust my intuition to lead the way

I replace my fear with trust that life is FOR me

I am worthy of al the joy and love that everyone else has around me

Feeling like a Victim: I Create My Life

As I write this chapter, I am thinking about compassion. When things happen in my life that I'm not prepared for, I can understandably feel like a victim of circumstances. As a mom, this feeling shows up for me when my thinking drifts into thoughts like "My *children* have messed up my day" or "My husband's mood has now put me in a bad mood." Sometimes I hear myself thinking, "Why does this always happen *to* me?" or "It's *your* fault." It's easy to blame everyone else for something going on in my life.

Several years ago, when I was in my height of feeling like a victim in my life, I actually felt a sense of relief believing that what was happening *to* me was out of my control. That meant I didn't have to take responsibility for it! It wasn't my fault. Besides, I got all kinds of attention for what I was going through. Friends would rally around me, letting me know that I was wronged by something in life. That felt pretty good, connecting and establishing bonds in this way. And I loved telling my story of woe.

How do we get out of this pattern of believing that we are victims in life and instead learning to take the wheel of our life? First, as long as we believe that we're victims, we will be victims. Remember that what we believe is what we perceive. This idea will weave itself throughout our children's lives as well. Shifting a belief system from "I am a victim" to "I am powerful and I create my own experience" will jump-start the process of change immediately.

Second, we moms need to have compassion for ourselves. That's why I am feeling such compassion as I write these words. There is a reason why a person feels like a victim, and it's because something painful has happened and it's too hard to see my part or my lesson. We deflect the pain by blaming others. Before anything else, feel compassion for yourself. Self-love is so important! If I don't think I'm worthy of good in my life, then I'm going to attract situations and people that will agree with me, or who feel the same unworthiness in themselves.

A Mother's Manual for Self-Love

You will easily find friends who will agree to your victimhood and they will tell their stories of being a victim as well. Victim energy is such an easy one to attract. Finding friends who see you in your power - now that is a friend who sees the real you.

Finally, it's important to realize that there is a power inside of you that has everything that you could ever need. It has the answers, it has the way and it has your power, ready for the taking. You can call it wisdom, god, intuition, fire, energy, spirit – whatever works for you. But, it is right there inside of you, as you read this book – there is nothing to look for outside of yourself. Bring your awareness to it. Close your eyes, calm your mind, and feel how alive you are!

You have the power to create your life as you want it.

Feeling like a victim in life is a false belief that tells you that everything happens *to* you and that you have no power over your life and your choices. The truth is that you have the power to create your life as you want it – you just need to *believe* in that power.

The Law of Attraction is a spiritual law that says what I believe is what I will see in my life. My life is a mirror of my thoughts. If I believe I am a victim, than I will see that belief reinforced in everything that I do. If I believe I am not worthy, I will attract people and situations to me that will prove my thoughts to be true.

Picture your beliefs as seeds. So thoughts like, "I'm not good enough, I'm always taken advantage of, and the world is against me, are each different examples of seeds that can be planted in your mind garden. Every time you think these thoughts, the seeds are watered, and they grow showing up stronger and stronger in your life experience. If you are planting a garden with seeds of victimhood and unworthiness, these seed-beliefs will grow into full-fledged victim-plants, and you will cultivate more experiences of the same pain and unhappiness in your life. Why not choose to plant your garden with beliefs of love, and with seeds of worthiness and freedom and power? See those love-plants and worthiness-plants sprouting up in your life instantaneously. Just by bringing your awareness to this truth about your life, you can begin to create a new way of being – and a new, more enjoyable life-garden to tend to.

Imagine that you are part of a much bigger part of life – that you are connected to everything and everyone and that you have the power to change everything in your life by changing your thoughts from victim to empowerment - because you are the decision-maker. You have the power within you to choose what happens next in your life. So, what would you change? How would that feel? Can you feel the power inside of yourself, just imagining the possibility? Can you feel how you are the center of your life and that you make the decisions for your life? Well, this is who you are! You are created with everything that you need to live a purposeful, inspired life.

Maybe you feel challenged about connecting to the inner self that holds all of your answers. First, I believe that this inner you – this inner light has never been touched by any pain, and doesn't know any victim thinking. It only knows love for you. That might be hard for you to see or feel right now, as you just start opening up to feelings its existence. Maybe the realization is buried in blankets of your past experiences. The way I began this journey was to use meditation and affirmations everyday. As you begin this daily routine, there may be a part of you that doesn't quite believe that this inner light is inside of you. The victim part of the ego can be very strong and not ready to let go! As you meditate, it might whisper, "You *are* a victim, you poor thing... the world is against you ... you aren't strong enough to do this..."

Silence that voice by affirming that you are *stronger* than any victim belief. And tell your victim consciousness, "You are no longer needed. Thank you for your services. From this point on, I move into every experience I have with my deep, intuitive inner power." Weed your garden and remove those victim plants.

A Mother's Manual for Self-Love

There are some valuable self-love lessons in the back of this book, so please read them if you are having trouble silencing that victim-voice. Remember, you are the *creator* of your life! You have the choice to feel good or not. You have the choice to stand in your power or not. You have the choice to be free or not. You have it all! Until you are aware of this power, nothing will change. Each of us is filled with the light energy of life. It's yours for the taking!

Affirmations for Creating Your Own Life

Life happens through me, not to me.

I release blame and take responsibility for my life.

I release the need to make everyone wrong around me.

I am empowered and made with purpose. I attract situations that prove my power and purpose.

I choose to live a victim-free life.

I ignite my power within today. I choose how I show up in every situation. No one can change this.

I take responsibility for how I am when I am with my kids. I choose to remain centered and authentic when I am with them. I do not give away my power.

Every situation in my life has brought me to where I am today. I am grateful for whatever that looks like.

I have compassion for myself and I know that I am perfect just as I am.

No situation in my life is stronger than my inner-self.

Gossip: I Release Unhealthy Judgment to Find Joy

"Jen thinks her son does everything perfectly – I can't believe she didn't say anything to him when he hit my daughter!"

"She spoils her kids way too much! They will have no idea how to manage when she's not around!"

Have you ever shared this kind of comment with a friend, or thought it to yourself? I've had friendships that seemed to be grounded on gossip – especially when I first became a mom and I was trying to figure out who I was in this new role. It can be addicting! I felt like I had no personal foundation, and had lost my identity in this new job of taking care of my child. I had no clue who *Michelle* was at the time.

Talking about other people was one thing that let me forget about how lost I felt in my own life. And if I was lost, how could I allow anyone else to have a clue to her identity or even to have a good life? I remember times when I left time with friends that were based on the gossip ritual, and feeling a sort of "high" from the closeness that had just been established. It really felt like gossiping had created a real bond between us. But, by the time I got home, the "high" had changed into that horrible, lost feeling again. I couldn't stand who I was at the time because I had no inner awareness of what to do and I was gossiping which felt even worse. I remember thinking, "So, is this what being a mom is all about?"

When we gossip about anything, kids, parenting, other people, we have one goal in mind: to set ourselves apart so that we can feel better about who we are. We are looking for a kind of power when we feel powerless. Our feeling of powerlessness tells us that we need to see ourselves as better than this person, or more knowledgeable than that parent. We are in a false belief that we are alone and different and separate from everyone else. And, we are looking to bond with other people and this is an easy way to connect.

Gossiping with a friend only hurts *my* spirit. Gossip only separates me from myself. And it only magnifies *my* unhappiness or uncertainty. Can you see where the self-love comes in here? When we gossip, that is our signal that we are trying to hide or withdraw from something unhappy or uncertain in our own lives.

Choose authentic relationships to find connection and self-acceptance.

My urge to gossip stopped as soon as I realized how bad it felt. I used my inner compass and sure enough it led me away from gossip and towards the real issue, which was my own unhappiness. It can feel like an addiction though. Gossiping about others is actually fueled by the false belief that it's a normal part of friendship - it's quite the opposite. And it leaves me feeling alone and guilty and it leaves other people unable to trust me. It was very difficult to change at first, quite honestly. Some of my friendships were steeped in gossip. Would these friends accept me with the changes I was making, or would we have nothing in common now that our conversations were being redirected? Looking back, it was actually an easy transition, but in the moment it felt so difficult.

As the conversation changed, so did the people around me. New friendships entered my life with moms who were looking to go deeper. The gossip-based friendships just ended gently, with no hard feelings on either side. And some transformed with me. I now look for friendships that are supportive and all-inclusive. I look for people that see the good in themselves and their children. As I focus on this heart's desire for inclusion and trust, I learn to value myself more. A new "muscle" is being exercised - one called *self-acceptance*. It's never about the other person when we gossip – it's always about ourselves! I learned to see that whatever I was feeling the urge to gossip about was actually my own insecurity.

It was like a breath of fresh air when I had my first conversations with moms who were on the same page as I was. I felt recharged and happy to be a good friend.

33

The feelings of loss and powerlessness that I'd felt before were replaced with acceptance and allowing. Being busy cultivating positive relationships also helped me create a more balanced life. My new muscle of self-acceptance got stronger and became a more normal part of my every day life.

In new situations, you might feel the temptation to gossip - maybe if you move or your kids start a new school, and you don't know anyone. For some reason, gossiping can feel like an easy way to bond. Try and remember that you want healthy accepting friendships. And you can always pull yourself out of unhealthy friendships for you and/or your family.

Of course, there are times when we all need to vent. It's been a tough day with the kids, or with a relationship, or we feel off and need to complain or simply download. However, what is different here is that - with a positive friendship - my friend believes in me and is not judging me when I might need to complain She also won't think less of me, or of the person I am bringing into the conversation, And, she wants me to feel better and she doesn't have the desire to make the other person wrong. She is listening confidentially, openly and lovingly. We won't venture into a bashing session about a relationship or the kids or whatever the stressor might be about. We can honor each other even when we need to vent. What a beautiful way to have friends. What a beautiful way to model relationships to our children.

Staying away from gossip is a continually working process. If you need some guidelines to help move away from gossip, here are two rules I try very hard to abide by when in conversation:

- When you bring up another person in a conversation – talking about them in a positive or negative way - you are often speaking *for* the other person, representing who they are, what they think, and what they stand for. For me, it's not comfortable to speak *for* someone, or to bring up their private business. Because I no longer choose to gossip, my gut tells me when

34

I've strayed into speaking for another human being.

- If you're going to talk about someone who is not in the room, act as if they *are* in the room. If you'd feel uncomfortable making a certain comment or sharing information in front of that person, that's a clear sign that you are entering the gossip realm.

As soon as you admit that you get some kind of feel-good result from the habit of gossip, you are already creating space that allows something new to replace it. Open yourself to a new agreement, where you find joy in genuine, gossip-free alliances. Realize you are using gossip to hide from your own unhappiness, and that this is a pattern in your behavior that can be changed. Then, create a vision of what kind of friends you want to attract. Finally, be that vision of the good friend. Walk in that vision and those loving, accepting, nonjudgmental friends will find you. And above all, if you find yourself getting into gossip again, be kind to yourself and start over.

Affirmations like the ones below will help imprint in your mind that you are absolutely perfect just as you are. You can find the truth that says you can release judgment, and feel good about *yourself* and other moms.

Affirmations to Release Judgment and Find Joy

I send love and compassion to myself and to all parents.

I am one with all life, so I am one with all parents.

What is right for me is not necessarily right for anyone else. I release all judgment of other mothers and fathers.

I accept myself where I am right now. I am here on purpose to be the woman and the mother I am meant to be.

I send love to (name the person in your life) and release all judgment or urge to gossip that I've felt in the past.

Because I am one with all life, I am equal to every person I meet. No one is better than or less than me.

I am one with self-love, unconditional love, acceptance and allowing. I am one with sacred connection and communion with friends.

I connect to the spirit in every person I meet. I see the bigger picture and send love to everyone I meet.

Guilt: I Let Go and Life Happen

Two of my children were born early – not too early but early enough to require them to stay in the neo-natal intensive care unit for just over a week. My thoughts were: "It's my fault. I should have done something differently. Did I worry myself into this? Could I have stopped this from happening?"

When I left the hospital without my first daughter, leaving her to the care of strangers, it was gut-wrenching for me. Unable to hold her, bring her home, feed her, or take care of her, I felt a guilt that was truly overwhelming.

My son has serious seasonal allergies that have now shifted to last for about one month each year in the spring. He receives allergy shots and we prepare each March hoping that this year, he will have some relief. Each year he suffers. He misses several days of school, he ends up rubbing his face so much he loses skin and is red and raw. He closes himself up in a dark room with no noise because of severe headaches and body aches. He takes double doses of just about everything, we've tried holistic options and nothing seems to help until we put him on a steroid, or time passes and he feels better. He suffers. And I feel guilty. Allergies run in my family. Even though I know better, I feel guilty.

I hear about guilt from mothers who have careers out of the home and feel that they should be spending time with their kids. Or stay-at-home moms who feel guilty because they are with their children all of the time and they feel like they need a break. Other moms feel guilty that they're doing too much, or not enough, or if they take some time for themselves, they're somehow being selfish. We feel guilt about how we handle our daily interactions with our kids.

I've actually felt that I *deserved* to feel guilty because it's just part of being a mom. We moms have been taught to accept a critical false belief that says, "Moms are supposed to feel guilty and we are deserving of punishment – it's part of the job!"

So Moms, this is my suggestion: You and I are going to feel guilty, and that's okay. What you do with that guilt is the important part. I use guilt for the reason it is there in the first place - it's a "signal". When I get the guilt signal, here's what I do:

- I breathe.

- I recognize my honest, *true* part in the situation.

- I see my part and learn from this guilt. If I'm taking on guilt that is not mine to bear, I accept that as truth. I let myself be free of it. If it is mine, I see my part.

- I use my hindsight, my inner wisdom to learn from the whole situation and then I choose to move forward.

- I let the guilt go.

Let go of guilt and let life happen.

If my child was born prematurely, is there anything I can learn from that to do it differently next time? Not really. So, I take in the awareness that I couldn't have changed the outcome. I accept what is happening and ask for guidance about how to move forward. There is a bigger picture that I can't see now, and might not ever see.

At one point I shared something private about my child with a mom. A while later my child came home very angry with me. He told me that the mom shared the private thing with him. He was so upset. I felt very guilty. I used the guilt as a signal. I owned it. I apologized. And I acknowledged my part. I had shared something that I shouldn't have. I took this moment as a lesson and learned to keep my kids' lives private.

Maybe you're feeling guilty because you can't be home with your kids as much as you'd like. Is there something you could do differently? Maybe not. Passions or life circumstances might be keeping you away so that is what you do. And are we allowed to enjoy our careers?

A Mother's Manual for Self-Love

Yes! It's not selfish to have a passion/career outside of the family! Whatever your choice or situation or family circumstance has you doing, own it. What is best for you is also best for every one in your family.

When you get triggered by your children and say things that later bring guilt, is there anything you can learn from that? Yes. Turn loving attention onto yourself. You need it. No more bad-mouthing yourself! Be an unconditionally loving voice that only knows love for you. And it's a perfect time to check in and go through the 5 steps above. Love yourself before you interact with your kids. You can remind yourself that you are safe, loved and protected, visualizing before you are even around your child that you are in a place of peace. When you take care of yourself, you naturally know what to do next with your children.

Each situation that guilt comes into is an opportunity to learn and move on as the mom and as the child. We each learn about healthier boundaries and ownership.

No matter what your responsibilities or your choices, you are living the perfect life for you and for your family. Remember, that what is best for you is best for your family. Once you can accept that, you can start living in freedom and remove the chains of guilt that you have attached to yourself. You are the perfect, whole, incredibly gifted person that is *mother*. Let go of guilt and breathe in freedom.

Moms, let go and let life happen. You are human. Let yourself be. Remember that one of your life's purposes is to be in joy. Allow for this. Let go of the weight of guilt so you can be free. I believe your child chose you to be his mother. Breathe that in and know that all is well.

Affirmations to Let Life Happen

I forgive myself now and I let go.

The source of my being is unconditional love. I align with that and move through this day in this awareness.

39

A Mother's Manual for Self-Love

I am an individual incarnation of spirit made for a specific purpose. I am as special as the most special person I know.

I am alive and fully activated in the present moment, letting go of anything that keeps me in the past or the future.

I close the chapter of the past and begin a new one today. My new chapter is sourced with unconditional love and forgiveness.

I am the perfect mother for my child, exactly as I am, and doing exactly what I am doing,

I release any old belief system that guilt is love. I allow my life to flow in freedom and I trust that what is good for me is also good for my whole family.

Helplessness: When we hurt for our child. I am Present

When we hurt for our children, It's an indescribable emotion. It's worry, fear, sadness, panic, despair, and even more - all rolled into one. It's helplessness. It feels like it will never go away. We can make ourselves sick when we are in this state - it can become all-consuming. Being in this heavy sadness can lead to anxiety, stress, obsessive thoughts, anger, exhaustion, depression, lack of sleep, and other physical ailments. No person can understand this emotion unless they are a parent.

When I have felt this unnamed emotion, it's time to practice HUGE mental control. Imagination and story telling can take over. Let's say something has happened in my child's life and he or she is desperately sad. Here I am, sending my child out into the world and I don't trust any part of what he/she will experience that day. The lack of control can feel suffocating. Seeing our children struggle and feel pain can be gut wrenching. There is no way to put a bow on this. There *are* some things that you can do to support you though, through the process. Moms - we need to stay healthy so we can be that strong, unconditionally loving place for our children. Here are some simple ideas that will help you remain that force for your kids.

1. In your mind, create a trust in your child. Remind yourself that growing up is sometimes extremely hard and painful. Get your affirmative thoughts going throughout the day, "I trust that my child is exactly where he is supposed to be, I trust that he will get through this learning what he needs to learn, I have every confidence that this will pass and he will be stronger because of it." The more you can do this, the better your energy will be when you are face to face with your child. Trust in your child's process - no matter what it looks like.

2. The moment you realize you are story telling in your thoughts (telling the story over and

over, creating stories that make you more scared and make the situation even more dramatic), pull yourself out of that by staying present and saying out loud what you can see in front of you (I see a black kitchen counter and a glass of water, etc) what you can feel (I feel the kitchen stool beneath me, the counter top is cold on my hands,) and what you can hear (I hear my dog walking across the floor, I hear the wind on the house, I hear the toilet flush,). Continue this process until your thoughts have shifted.

3. Allow yourself to share your story to a trusted friend. Then try not to tell it again. Sharing our story over and over only reinforces it. It keeps it high on our minds and it makes more room for people to participate in the judging/gossiping area. If you can keep this situation between just a couple of people who you trust that will see the highest good for you, your child and the other people involved, you will end up with a much more balanced, healthy outcome in the end.

4. Put the question out there: "What can I do to support my child?" Ask this question out loud and then wait for an answer. One of the hardest parts about having a child in distress is that we feel like our hands are tied. We can't make it go away. We CAN be there as the unconditionally loving support that they need. I have found that whenever I ask this question I get direction. Maybe it's from a friend who I've shared this with, or an idea, or maybe the direction is to be present and available for my child. When you can trust yourself, you will feel more confident in your next steps.

5. It's not your fault. Struggles are a part of life. You are the exact right person to be there for your child. Trust this about yourself. If you feel guilty, figure out why and then make

42

a conscious effort to make a change. Then let the guilt go. It doesn't help anyone, especially you.

6. Trust in your parenting. Do what feels right to you. Sometimes you will get feedback from others that really sounds good to you. Sometimes the feedback won't resonate. Always remember to stay true to yourself and what is best for you and your family.

7. This to shall pass. In the heat of the moment life can feel like a snail's pace. Remind yourself that this will pass. You will feel good again. You will get through this.

Affirmations To Be Present When You Feel Helpless

1. I am the exact right person to be my child's parent.

2. I am alive, awake and aware to the present moment.

3. I trust that no matter what it looks like, my child is on his/her perfect right path.

4. I trust in my child's process. I don't judge it. I allow for it to be.

5. This too, shall pass.

I am Not My Mother: I Accept and Forgive

Okay, this is hard to write for fear of my own mother taking it very personally - although I don't know any mom who hasn't said these words at some point in her life! It's human nature to want to do things our own way. Many of our childhood experiences were wonderful. There are also many things that we hope to do as well as our parents. I want to share about those mom-things that you swore to yourself –even as a child – that you would *never* do, often because they changed the pattern of your behavior in a negative way. The fears that grew in us as a result of these changes can also be very deep-rooted, affecting decisions we make for our children.

My friend Karen told me that her mom went through a few divorces, and whenever her mother would get upset with her husband-at-the-time, she would send Karen and her sisters to the car. Karen would watch her mom walk out of the house with boxes packed and then see her house vanish in the distance as her mother drove her and her sisters away. Karen is afraid of marriage now, and fearful about having children because she thinks she'll do the same thing.

Another friend, Stephanie, remembers a certain look that her mother would give her that felt so full of hate and disapproval. She remembers feeling afraid of her mom, like she was supposed to love her, but it was scary to love her. Stephanie says that she put up walls around her to remain emotionless, so she wouldn't be affected by the hatred she felt from her mom. Today she never wants her own child to experience what felt like being hated by her mom. So, she doesn't let herself get angry around the children, which is causing her some health issues.

We see parents today putting their kids in class after class, hoping their children can find a specific interest and become an expert at it. I've heard people say that they do this because *their* parents didn't put them in anything. Or that their parents exposed them to a lot of things, but never helped them find a specific interest.

44

A Mother's Manual for Self-Love

There is a false belief here that if I do the complete opposite of my mother, then I can create a better experience for my family. The truth is, what I resist will persist in my life. I need to accept, forgive, and move on from my past, so that I can create a brand new, neutrally charged pattern for my family. When I rebel against my childhood I am not being authentic because I am only 'reacting' to something that happened in my life. When I accept my life for the way it was and I make decisions from *that* space, I am authentic and my past will not persist in my life.

Accept the past and forgive with compassion so you can move on to making your choices from a place of freedom.

There is much that we learned from our parents that we want to take into our own families– like memories and traditions that we hold onto and cherish. And, in other areas, we might hope for life to be different. No matter what, our parents received patterns from their parents, and so on. That means that there are unconscious patterns repeating all along your ancestral line.

As children, we take these patterns in. We leave our homes and believe we have it all figured out. We say, "I will never do (fill in the blank)". Then, when we have children, we are faced with a new, unfamiliar situation. More is required of us at a much faster pace, so in moments that we are not present or conscious, we might fall right into those "I'll never do that" patterns without even realizing it. And then we loathe ourselves for replaying the same past experience we swore we'd never do.

My friend Karen, who got packed up in the car every time her mom left one of her husbands, says she feels a kind of comfort in packing up boxes when she and her husband get into a fight. She says that she wants to ignore her past, to forget about being that little girl in the car and just move on. Today, she works hard at being happy and loving with her husband, but when they get into a fight, she is ready to leave and she can't figure out why.

Another friend of mine, Dana, felt very controlled in an abusive way when she was young. Later, as the mother of a four year-old daughter, Dana's parenting consisted of allowing her daughter to be as free as possible. In other words, her four year-old ran her home! In order to rebel against her past, Dana went to the opposite extreme. So, when deep anger came up for her, she couldn't figure out why. She wanted to be free and loving but she kept having fits of out-of-control anger – which is what can happen when we rebel against our past rather than accepting it, forgiving it and moving on. Dana has worked through this now, and she has shifted her parenting style to something more proactive and more from a neutral space within her.

How can we move from rebelling against our childhood to being able to make clear cut, neutral decisions for our family? First, write down *your* story. Let it all out on paper. When we write down our memories and the feelings they bring up, we make them real and we create an outlet for them. Write down the experiences that you are so afraid of re-creating. Then, see if you can figure out how this is showing up in your life today. Where are you overcompensating for something in your past? Are you afraid of your anger? Are you afraid of being too strict so you parent with no boundaries and find yourself losing it with your child? Or is it the opposite, are you creating an overly controlled environment because you don't feel you had any direction as a kid?

Next, it's important to see your own parents through compassionate eyes and to forgive them. This will help you let go of your past. Take a moment to see your parents in their full story. Was your mom a single mom, or a mom that had no support from family? What was her life like growing up? Were her parents supportive? Was your mom secure or insecure? How much responsibility was on her plate? Write out this story from your mother's perspective. Realize that your mother is a human being that has lived her life with different experiences than you have. And that she did the best she could at the time and with the knowledge that she had. See your mother through compassionate eyes. And when you are ready, forgive her. Let her go from this memory. When you can forgive your mother, you can begin to forgive yourself, for anything that you have done or said or felt, that you regret.

Here's an example:

Looking back: *I remember being so controlled as a child. I wasn't allowed to do anything. I remember my mom telling me that I couldn't do anything I wanted to do because it was for my own good. I sat in my room and fantasized about when I would get out of there. She didn't trust that I would make the right choices so she never let me spend the night at friends or go to parties. I felt like an outcast – like I would never fit in with all the other kids.*

How it shows up now: *I let my daughter make her own choices. She is carefree but I now realize that she is running the show. She acts out all of the time, throwing tantrums when she has to do something that she doesn't want to do, and she is seven years old. I find myself holding in my anger and then flying off the handle – using the same angry voice and hateful eyes I remember from my mom. But I refuse to be controlling so I don't know what to do.*

Compassion for my mother: *My mom was a single parent. Her sister died when she was very young, leaving my mom feeling very vulnerable. She wanted to control my every move so she could feel safe. I bet she was controlled by her parents as well. There was probably a lot of sadness in her family when her sister passed away. She was only trying to protect me in the only way she knew how. I know how that feels – I don't want anything bad to happen to my kids. I can understand the fear a mother can have.*

Forgiveness: *I forgive my mom. I know she did the best she could. I pray that my children have the same compassion for me that I have for my mom. I release her and I let the experiences go. I now move forward from a place of freedom.*

If there is one thing you take from this chapter I hope it is how important it is to *forgive* or let go. This doesn't have to be a religious experience if you are not a religious person. When I hold onto something from my past, I am keeping my consciousness there – in the past. So, even though the experience is long over, I am still there in the past. When I can let go of the past by using compassion, and release myself from it, I am free to be me, in this moment. I start my day with a clean slate when I let go of the things from my past that were painful.

I hope that you can do this too! I hope for you that you can let go and move forward in your own perfect time. Your parenting will shift immediately. And the more compassionate you are with people from your past, the more compassionate you will be with yourself. I pray for you that the rebellion ends, the resistance stops, and you can shine through in your authentic nature.

Affirmations to Accept and Forgive My Mother and My Past

I forgive and I let go of any anger that I am holding onto about my mother.

I move forward in freedom from this moment on.

I am compassionate towards my mother and her experiences in life and, in turn, I am compassionate with myself.

I accept my past knowing it got me to where I am now.

I am free and clear now.

I am grateful for all of my life experiences!

I see with fresh eyes!

It's Just the Way it is: I Choose My Unique Experience

"Here it comes. Brian's home from work with stomach flu and it's only a matter of time before it goes around the whole house." Or, "Strep throat is going around and I always get strep throat!" Or, "John always gets so sick in January – it's just his month." "She is always a mess – she always leaves everything out – "that's just what we expect from him - such a disappointment!" "There she goes again!" "January is always hard with us being stuck inside."

When I believe these blanket statements about life, I make myself vulnerable. But, what is amazing to realize is that I have a choice to believe those thoughts, or to create new beliefs that benefit me and my family. For example, some general popular beliefs are, "It's so hard to get into a good public school in the city... I'll never get a parking spot in front of the kids' music class... When one of us gets the stomach flu we all get it...all boys are aggressive...all girls are so dramatic and emotional... The kids in that neighborhood are all so spoiled...Teenaged girls are impossible!...I'm just a mom!"
Beliefs like these are experienced and held as the truth by many of us, and some have been perceived as the *last word* for generations and generations of mothers.

Now, picture all of the statements that have ever been believed by moms around the world for generations as little "balloons". Those little balloons (our false beliefs) have taken over the world. They fill our neighborhoods, our homes, our cars, our conversations, our books and our airwaves. Since we see these false belief balloons everywhere we are, we think of them as real. Over time, we even add our own false belief balloons. Every time I say, "Everyone is getting sick now because it's winter, so I'm just waiting for the other shoe to drop", I'm adding my own little balloons to the mix.

But here and there, there are moms who are popping these false belief balloons, one balloon at a time, by changing the pattern in their homes. The truth is we don't have to buy into these beliefs. We can break free from old, unhealthy thought patterns and create new ways of perceiving our experiences that *serve* our wellbeing.

What we believe is what we will experience in our lives.

When I lived in Chicago my garage wasn't attached to the house. When getting home in the dark, I went through the same internal dialogue. A few blocks before my house I'd start saying, "Oh my gosh, I'm sure that someone is waiting in the garage, I'm sure that someone is waiting on the deck to attack me. I was completely panicked by the time I pulled into the garage. My heart would be pounding and my blood pressure would be up. One particular evening, I went through that process and as I opened the garage door I saw something out of the corner of my eye and I was absolutely certain it was someone. I screamed a scream that would have terrified anyone nearby and I ran into my house. I then realized it was a big stack of out door chairs I had put there earlier in the day. My emotions, my mental state and my body all had the experience of me being attacked – even though nothing was there. Did I get attacked? No. Did I create a situation because of my belief that I would be attacked? Yes.

If I believe that every winter brings on colds and flu viruses, then that's what I'll experience every winter. It will show up in actual illnesses or worry and fear that illnesses are coming. But, think about it. Illnesses do not *have* to be passed around. There are plenty of families who have children that don't get sick. There are families chosen in the school lottery every year whose children get into public school. Someone is getting those front row parking spots. And we know that not all boys are aggressive, and not all girls are emotional time bombs by the time they enter high school.

When a false belief balloon shows up in my life saying, "Oh no, I know what's coming", or "Everybody else thinks it's true", I can check myself and claim the truth that my experience is authentically *mine*. I can pop that balloon. My path has never been walked by anyone else, so it won't look the same as anyone else's path. Even if it was the truth of last winter, it doesn't' predict my current one. That's a very powerful place for each of us to be – to know that we can agree with whatever we choose to agree with. And, most importantly, that we can choose to pop those false belief balloons whenever it's right for us.

Have you heard the saying, "Change your thinking, change your life"? This concept is very important as you go through life as a parent. It's also a powerful statement that might bring up thoughts like, "Uh oh, now I have to take responsibility" or "I can't be a victim of circumstances anymore." But the truth is, as you start working with what the statement is telling you, you begin to realize just how much your thoughts have been affecting your *perception* of what was happening. Even if nothing changes in the experience, if you change your perception, your experience of what is happening will be completely different.

For example, driving around saying to yourself, "I never get parking spots", is going to put you in a non-receptive place where you might pass up a parking spot opening up right where you needed one. At the very least, you know you'll be miserable as you drive around and around looking for a spot with that negative thinking pulling you down. Instead, try driving around saying, "I have everything I need, and I know I'll get a parking spot today". That puts you in a different frame of mind. And even if you need to drive around a bit, you will find a spot and you will be happier looking for it! You have the same experience, but you perceive it very differently.

If I put my energy into a false belief, then that is what will show up in my experience. However, if I claim my experience as easy and effortless, and I truly believe it, than it will be so. When I realized this truth, I felt so free that I started making rituals to support my new way of thinking. Imagine waking up in the morning, lighting a candle while getting breakfast ready, and starting your day with, "Our home is filled with vitality and light and love. Today the kids are in balance and their bodies and minds are safe and protected", or "I know that health and wholeness thrives in my house. No sickness passes between our family members." These affirmations help me to deflate any of those "false belief balloons" and have made a very big difference in our family dynamic. We haven't passed along an illness to every member of the family since I began doing it.

Another ritual that I love is something called *sage smudging*. Sage smudging is the ancient Native American practice of burning a bundle of sage and using the aromatic smoke to clear out the energy of bad feelings/bad energy or their influences. So, I choose to do this in my home when things aren't feeling quite right. I smudge through my house when the kids get into phases of waking up a bunch of times during the night, or when I've had a rough day myself, or anytime I'm looking for a fresh start! For me, sage smudging makes it feel like our home had a bath. There's also immediate relief when I sage to help the kids stay in bed at night. Rituals are great ways to make your day sacred and important. Enjoy creating your own rituals – your own unique experiences - that get you to a place of feeling confident and assured that all is well.

Affirmations to Affirm My Own Unique Experience

I consciously live my life, choosing beliefs that support my growth and the growth of my family.

I let go of limiting beliefs that do not serve me.

I ask my intuition to highlight any limiting beliefs that I am not aware of.

I walk in the light of authentic living with no attachment to what other people think.

I only allow beliefs to enter my home that are for the highest good of my family.

Any limiting beliefs that feel too big to dissolve on my own, I offer them now to Spirit, knowing that there is no order in the difficulty of miracles. Spirit doesn't judge my

miracle as being harder or impossible to accomplish –
only I do that. Spirit only says yes.

Jealousy: I'm happy for her and I am open to the same thing happening for me

Jennifer Garner. She is what comes up for me. I've never been jealous where I don't like her, but more jealous because to me, she seems to have *everything*. And I feel like she has such a great platform to teach moms how to love and take care of themselves. And she does it! I've read interviews with her saying she thinks we need to be kinder to each other. Sometimes though, when I'm looking at her big powerful life and dreaming of having it, my life starts to feel small and deflated.

Does that ever happen to you? Do you have any neighbors or friends that you imagine have it all? You might feel jealous thinking, "I'll never have all of that!" Or sometimes you might think, "Their kids have it made!" It can sometimes be stifling to feel jealous. Because there is a false belief that says "I can't ever have what they have." "I'll never have that life." And another thought is, "What they have is way better and more balanced and normal than what I have." Or another belief is, "There is only room for *her* to have that – so I never will." We start to feel very separate from everyone when we feel this way. Like we aren't good enough to have what the other person has. "That is for *other* people."

Sometimes when we feel jealous we then talk about the person to make us feel better. This absolutely happens in kids, and I've definitely felt it and seen it in adults as well. "Can you believe how much money she wasted on that new car?" or " She is in such good shape, it's almost like she spends too much time at the gym." Or, "Her husband is so good to her it's annoying." Or, "everyone has *something* going wrong in their lives. I'm sure *something* is going on behind her closed door!"

So if our thoughts are things, and help shape our lives, what are we doing when we make these comments about people we are jealous of? We are actually pushing away everything that we are jealous of from happening in our own lives. Even if these things were in our lives, we wouldn't see them because we are too busy pushing them away and making them wrong.

Jealousy is all about living in a world of hierarchy. The belief is that there are people who are better than and more deserving than me. And I will never have what they have. And this is absolutely not true.

It's not what someone else *has* that we are jealous of. It's what we think having that thing makes them *feel* like that we are jealous of. So I admit that I sometimes feel jealous of Jennifer Garner. She has a career, a family, no financial issues, she's gorgeous, and she apparently decorates like Martha Stewart. And, she supports moms. What it really comes down to is that I am jealous of her solid purpose in life. If you are feeling jealous about someone's healthy body, you are probably feeling jealous of the time she has to work out, or the commitment she makes, or the positive energy that she probably has. If it's about someone getting a new car, it's probably more about the financial freedom that you believe the person might have. And if it's about the husband that seems perfect, that is more about the connection that you might be missing in your own relationship.

For me, when I start to feel small or deflated because of someone else's success, I pinpoint what it is I'm actually jealous of, and I try and bring that into my life. So with Jennifer having a solid purpose in her life, I ask myself, "how can I have a solid purpose in my life?" I also start listing the things that I *have* accomplished. It might be that I pick up a song I was writing and finish it. Or I might add something to my blog. I might spend some time organizing my home so I can feel that sense of comfort that a home brings. If I'm feeling jealous about someone getting a new car, I can clean and organize my own car so it feels new and taken care of. The goal here is to realize that we are all human beings and we all feel the same feelings. So you can create in *your* life, what someone else has in his or hers. If you take the time to figure out what you are *really* feeling jealous of, you will realize it's something that you can attain in your own life.

We can't make other people wrong for living their true lives. When we do that, we push ourselves further away from living our own true lives. What we can do is put our attention on what it is we feel we are missing and with baby steps, call in the same joy that we think someone else has.

" I am happy for her and I am available to have the same if not more in my life."

Affirmations for "I am open to receiving all of my good"

There is room for everyone to have joy in their lives.

I use my jealousy is a mirror. I activate my life NOW with the thing I am jealous of.

I can have it all!

I am equal to everyone that I know. No one is better than or less than me.

Judgment: I Choose Compassion

We all judge to some extent. Whether it's judging whether or not to wear shorts when the temperature is 50degrees or deciding that I'm a horrible person because I yelled at my kids today - judgment happens. Most of the time, judgment is very good for us. We need to decide how to be safe and live a responsible happy life and we do that by judging our options and making the best ones. When used correctly, healthy judgments are driven by your instincts. The definition of judgment is, "the ability to make considered decisions or come to sensible conclusions." The type of judgment that I'm talking about in this chapter is the kind that keeps us small. It's probably seen more as "hyper" judgment.

Judgments towards ourselves

The first time I had guests over after having my first child, I felt the need to be put together and look like I was a perfect mom. But, how did I feel inside? Lousy! I felt like a sleep-deprived mess. I had no idea what I was doing, and was even scared that I was going to starve my child. I felt like the only mom whose instincts didn't kick in - as everyone told me that they would! Yet, here I was, getting myself ready to look perfect for the guests we had coming over.

I was judged myself as wrong for how I was actually feeling. Then I was masking this "wrongness" by being the complete opposite. I had made a judgment call that I needed to be "perfect" in order to be a good mom. Yet here I was, an insecure, crumbling-on-the-inside new mother with a smile on my made-up face, welcoming our guests.

I've sometimes judged myself very harshly throughout my years of being a mom. I'm not good enough, I'm not social enough, I'm not fun enough, etc... I find that these judgments happen when I start comparing myself to everyone "out there." I have forgotten who I am. I'm deciding who I am based on the judgments I've made about how other people are living *their* lives.

Judgments towards others

Healthy judgment helps us set appropriate boundaries around the people that we meet day to day. Will I let that person in or will I create a safe boundary? Our judgments about how we connect with people help us create balance in our lives. These tend to happen naturally, without our even knowing and without much discussion with others.

Unhealthy judgments begin when we judge most people in our lives as wrong, bad, better than, less than, smarter, prettier, lesser, perfect, etc. We are unconsciously building an infrastructure of hierarchy so every person has a place. We are probably all aware of what this looks like when it's unhealthy. We are actually trying to make ourselves feel better by making someone else look bad. If you start feeling guilty or bad inside, for things that you are saying or someone is saying to you, you can use that as a guide that something is off.

Judgments towards life

Healthy judgments towards life keep us on a balanced path. We make wise choices and we listen to our gut instinct when we are faced with decisions.

Unhealthy judgments towards life tend to be very opinionated and they keep us away from our joy. We might feel like life is against us so when we meet new situations we go into them with that negative judgment. This can then affect the outcome, which then proves our "judgment" right. And the circle continues.

Why do we judge?

Most of the time, when we are "hyper" judging, it's because we are feeling attacked and insecure. For example, when we see someone doing something different than us we feel the need to make that person wrong so that we can stay right. Maybe we feel safe by placing labels on every person around us so that we can keep our place right where we are. We might feel competitive with someone and judging that person keeps me winning. We might have trouble admitting when our children mess up, so we blame the people around them instead. We might be bored. We might feel like it's the only way we can connect to a new friend or social group.

How to Judge in a healthy way

When you are establishing healthy boundaries in your life around anything at all, it's important to use your judgment, which when done in a healthy way is driven by your instincts.

Ask yourself these questions before you make a judgment about anything else:

1. What is my motivation?

2. Am I feeling like I'm in competition with someone?

3. Am I feeling attacked? Now, am I really being attacked?

4. Would I say this if (the subject) was in the room?

5. What is my part in this? (We always have a part)

Allow for people to be who they are. Allow for yourself to be who you are, where you are and remind yourself that you are important and valuable and making decisions just as important as everyone else's decisions. Remind yourself, that there is room for you and for everyone! List off 10 things about yourself that you love if you start to feel like you want to judge someone else. No one can take your light. We all have our own paths. If you feel attacked because someone is doing something different from you, remind yourself - that we are all here to learn from each other. No one is attacking you. You are safe and sound. There is room for all of us.

As parents, we need to find more compassion in our hearts for ourselves and the other people in our lives.

As parents, we are each doing the best that we can. We are each parenting from our own experience, beliefs and the knowledge that we have right now with the ultimate goal of raising happy children. So, let's start looking at each other as a team! All moms can stand together to support each other – and have both compassion for each other's mistakes and celebration for each other's joys knowing there is room for all of us. Do we need to all be best friends? No. Let's respect each other and trust that we are each doing the best that we can.

If you want to go deeper

When I am judging someone else, in an unhealthy way, I am actually not accepting something about myself. I am rejecting an aspect of ME. I wouldn't see the thing in the other person if it wasn't already in me (breathe!). My judgment about someone else is a mirror giving me a wonderful opportunity to have my own insecurity reflected back to me. Since judgment is all about not loving myself, I have to ask, "What it is in me that I am trying to hide from by moving the negative spotlight onto a different person?"

Example of a reaction to unhealthy judgment: Years ago, I had a friend who used to frustrate me with how she would talk badly about her other friends. I would go home after a visit with her, and complain to my husband about how disrespectful she was about her friends. I'd then call another friend the next day and tell her all about it. And then I tell another friend, and then another.

Same example but using strategies to keep it healthy: Years ago I had a friend who liked to talk badly about most of her friends. I'd leave her house feeling bad after our conversations. I tried to change the conversation but ultimately, we would end up sharing a lot of judgments about people. I talked with my husband about this- a safe person that I knew wouldn't add to the drama I was feeling. I clearly would get pulled in and would feel bad. I noticed that what bothered me in her was also in me. So I made some changes in myself and made conscious efforts not to participate in those types of conversations. Slowly, we found we didn't have that much in common and very naturally our relationship shifted.

A Mother's Manual for Self-Love

Here is another way to find compassion, which I've found to be very powerful. Let's say I get into judgment when someone cuts me off while I'm driving. I immediately say, "I forgive myself for any time that I cut someone off and didn't realize it." Wow! The first time I did this there was a huge release of tension. It brought me and the person that just cut me off together as *one*. The same kind of release came when I heard a mother say something to her child that I didn't agree with - "I forgive myself for any time I spoke disrespectfully to my child." If you find yourself judging someone who is talking negatively or gossiping, you can say something like, "I forgive myself for any time that I spoke negatively about anyone." If the forgiveness statement doesn't' quite resonate, pull it out a bit. If you judge a parent because she cut in front of you in traffic and you feel you always drive perfectly, you can't really say, "I forgive myself for any time I didn't drive perfectly." You *could* say, "I forgive myself for every time I haven't been perfect." And then just affirm inside yourself that perfection is about allowing yourself to be whoever you need to be in the moment.

If there is someone in your life that you keep struggling with judgment about, check out the "Healthy Boundaries" chapter for some tips on creating healthier relationships with the people around you.

What this practice does is create a space for "allowing". You are allowing yourself and others to be human. You are accepting every aspect of yourself. You are creating room for yourself and everyone else to be who they need to be. And you are creating healthy boundaries for you and your family. And when you accept every aspect of yourself, you love yourself more. You will then also be more allowing of your children and friends to be who they are.

Affirmations for Choosing Compassion

I am safe all the time.

There is room for everyone.

A Mother's Manual for Self-Love

I love and accept myself. I (love and) accept the person I am judging.

I see my part and I learn from it and move on.

There is room for me to be right and there is room for others to be right and different all at the same time.

What is right for me is right for me. I allow (instead of judge) for everyone to live their lives the way they are supposed to live them.

I allow my children and other children to be just as they are, and through this I am honoring their path. When I show up in "allowing", I am honoring my path in self-love.

I love and honor myself as mother to my children. I allow for my experience to be what it is. I accept every aspect of my parenting.

What I resist persists, so I allow any judgment to move through me and dissipate into the nothingness that they originally came from. I forgive myself and let go.

I create new wiring in my mind that is inclusive and allowing of all of my thoughts and all people that come my way.

Living in the Past or Future: I Live in the Now

I had just plopped down in the basement to play with my girls when the phone rang. It was my editor, so I took the call and afterwards I was over the moon with excitement. Even after I hung up the phone, I couldn't stop thinking about my book – this book!

I'm imagining how helpful this book is going to be to moms everywhere, and the new inspirational learning's I want to add. Then I remember that I left a load of laundry in the washer, so I ran upstairs to throw the clothes in the dryer. On my way upstairs I see that I didn't clean up after lunch, so I quickly put the dishes in the dishwasher. I then headed upstairs to take care of the laundry. As I opened the dryer, I'm imagining that someday I'll be speaking to moms shedding a much-needed light on how important it is for them to love themselves. Oops! There are clothes in the dryer that need to be folded... and I've made a decision that I won't leave folded clothes out in the hallway anymore, so I take the time to put all the folded clothes away.

I go in the girls' room and see that I haven't made their beds yet so I work on that. As I tuck in the cover, I'm planning the book release and the book signing in my mind. I head back downstairs, my head in the clouds thinking of my book. I pass the front door and realize I didn't get the mail yesterday so I go and get it. I go back to the basement and it hits me: "What was my original intention for the morning? Oh yes! Playing with my kids."

Almost 30 minutes had passed since the phone rang, and all awareness of my children had simply evaporated. They'd played on their own, but that was my time to be *with* them. Unfortunately, I was virtually nowhere to be found because I was living in the future.

When I am stewing over the past or musing about the future, I am covering up the present moment, the moment where life is. Sure, it felt good to be in my imagination, envisioning a wonderful future. It also felt good to get the housework done. But, that time had been allocated as "time with my kids", and I had missed those moments with them.

When I am in my head about something that happened earlier in the day or about something that might take place later, I am in the false belief that my thoughts about the past or future are *real* in the here and now. When I replay an earlier conversation with my friend or my husband, or when I take time to feel bad for something that happened to someone long ago, my attention is not in the here and now. And it's the same with daydreaming about something that might happen in the future. If I'm imagining an event next week or next month or next year, I am wishing my life away.

You show up as your authentic self when you are truly here, right now.

It's so easy to be in our heads, isn't it? To be totally present with our kids can feel difficult. Sometimes living in the now, right where you are, might feel uncomfortable or even boring. You might wish you were somewhere else, where you can forget about what's stressing you out. There are also times when the Now moment doesn't look very appealing at all, and going in your head lets you just numb out.

The truth is that it can be hard to let go of something from the past when there's no resolution. And when life seems dull or uncomfortable, it's tempting to daydream about a possible new life in the future. But, while living in the past or the future might feel like a getaway from your day, all you really get is lost time.

Acknowledging that your thoughts drift into the past or future is the first step in creating a space to change the habit. You begin by realizing that the only moment that is really happening is right now - right here in this moment. What can see, hear and touch: Here's an example from my own life.

I recently found myself getting ready to sing in front of a large audience. It's something I do fairly regularly, and my nerves typically run amok right before I go onstage.

We're talking *very* big butterflies! As I was sitting and waiting to sing, feeling my nerves starting to get the best of me, I said to myself, "I am sitting in this chair. I am wearing blue jeans and white shirt, and my husband Brian is sitting next to me." It clicked! I wasn't performing or messing up and forgetting my words - I was simply sitting in a chair next to my husband. When I got up to sing, I hadn't built up this huge story in my mind that I would forget my words, and guess what? I didn't!

It's a gift to realize - in the moment I am in – that nothing else is happening. My anticipation or daydreaming doesn't help. My worry doesn't aid me or the issue I'm facing. What helps and supports me is being in the now, where I am safe, connected and ready to hear any intuition that I need.

So moms, when you are with your kids, and you realize that your mind is distracted, just stop, focus and begin acknowledging everything in front of you. Then you can say, "I'm here. I'm sitting next to my child as she is drawing. The walls in front of me are beige. She is wearing pink shorts and a striped shirt. I feel the floor beneath me and I smell the scent of her socks." My thoughts and mind are totally in this now-present moment."

You will notice a significant shift in what you experience and accomplish. You become a better listener because you've stopped the internal chatter. You will find that answers come to you more quickly because of your focus. You will feel more fulfilled with the time you've had with your children, because you were *there* when you were with them. You will be calmer because you didn't spend your day over-thinking this or that experience in your life.

Remember and affirm: The only thing happening is right now. The only thing happening is right now. The only thing happening is right now.

Affirmations for Living in the Now Moment

I am in the Now moment. I breathe into this space and my mind remains here.

Everything gets clearer when I remain right here, right now. Answers flow to me effortlessly.

I am here now.

I let go of what is pulling me away from right here and right now.

All that is really happening in my life is right now. All that is really happening is right now. All that is really happening is right now.

I am fully present with my children right now- in body, mind and spirit.

I allow for my life to be right where it is, with no resistance.

The only thing happening is right now.

Making Comparisons: I Honor My Child

"Jack has been taking piano since he was three, and he's already doing recitals and performing in front of crowds".

"Stella has been in dance since she was a baby. We take her to the ballet and she just loves it."

"Steve is on the highest level soccer team and his parents give him private lessons."

Talking with other parents means we will be sharing a lot about our children. Sometimes these conversations bring up judgment about a parent or their child, or even about *my* child. Sometimes our children come home with comparisons to their friends. Competition can come into play, where we feel we need to brag about something our child has done so that we are "keeping up", or we feel bad because our child seems to fall short in comparison with other kids.

These moments of making comparisons are usually triggered when we are concerned that our child isn't doing the same thing or doing as well, or when we think the parent we're listening to is boasting. Either way, there is a false belief system here that declares, "When someone talks about how great their child is, they are saying that *my* child is not as great." It implies a kind of hierarchy system, and if your child is on top, then my child isn't.

Without even realizing it, I can fall into this false belief, thinking that there isn't room for my child to be just as wonderful as any other child. Then the self-doubt comes. How can my child be good enough if she isn't doing the same thing that this other child is doing? How can I not feel panicky if my child isn't being exposed to as much of "this" or "that" as her child? Does this mom I'm chatting with think my child isn't good enough? And, of course, I can worry immediately that I'm not doing as good a job as *that* parent because their child is involved in so many more things than my child.

Honor your child and yourself by remembering that all is one.

If you've ever fallen into this false belief, you probably felt separate from others as a child. That separateness is another false belief. Maybe you didn't feel good enough in high school, or maybe you felt superior in some way to other people. Today, you may feel the same less-than/better-than insecurities for your own children. Feeling separate from everyone else is actually a shield designed to keep you from showing up as your authentic self. Unfortunately, when you hold yourself apart from everyone else, you invite insecurity, sadness and feelings of hopelessness. That's because you are taking who you are and discounting it – making it not worthy.

A tough question that must be asked of ourselves as moms is, "Do we want our children to learn false belief from us?" Remember, you are one with all life. You are one with the person sitting across from you. You are one with the brilliance of the most brilliant person you know. You are one with the mom that you are judging to be so much better than you. And when you compare yourself as being less than someone else, you aren't participating in life as a fully alive human being.

So, check back in! Get back into life as a person who matters and makes a difference. See your gifts as important and necessary. See your life exactly as it is, and know that it is inspiring and as absolutely perfect. And if you are comparing your child to other children, realize that everything is okay. Where you are right now, you are okay. Your child is okay. He is enough. You are enough.

When we moved to a new town a few years ago, I was stunned by the differences in our daily activities when compared to Chicago. In my experience, the absolute focus of most families that we met was of their children's activities. We didn't experience this to this degree in Chicago. At first, I was excited for the change, and then I got scared. Kids were on travel teams for every sport – sometimes more than one. And if they hadn't started the travel team at a certain age, then chances are they would never be good enough to make a travel team later on. Kids were in music classes and on swim teams. One day I had talked with a few parents who had their kids on swim teams and I started to feel panicky that my children had barely taken swimming lessons. I came home and told my son that he was going to take swimming lessons so he could be part of a swim team. That was not very balanced and peaceful, right? He said he wasn't interested in being on a swim team and I said to him and I'm not kidding, "Well everyone else is on swim teams, Coop!" You know what he said to me? "Mom, I don't have to do what all of my friends are doing!" We need to release this need to compare and allow our kids to be who they are supposed to be!

When I compare my child to other kids, I am moving from fear. I remind myself that moving from fear isn't real. I take a deep breath. I listen. And I allow for my child to be exactly who he is supposed to be.

I was at a child's birthday party in Chicago a few years back, listening to some mothers talking about what high schools their kids had gotten into. Their children had tested to get into particular schools and all the kids, except for one, had gotten into the schools they wanted. I noticed that the mother whose son didn't get into his preferred high school was very quiet. Any comments she did make seemed laced with fear, worry, "not good enough" comments, and concern for her child, who'd been accepted into the next-best school on his list.

I sparked up a conversation with this mom, especially when I saw her concern and sadness for her son. She said he was devastated, and admitted that she had been comparing him to the other kids that made it into the "right" schools. She saw the whole process as a failure because what was "supposed" to happen instead fell through. We talked for awhile, and from my perspective as an outsider, this "failure" was actually an opportunity for her son to grow and express himself in a new environment.

I believe that our children call forth their perfect experience in life, so even though this next-best school outcome didn't seem right to her, it really was. It was important that she let go of comparisons and see that her son was being *called* to this other fantastic school. Eventually, she shared that the sports program was better at the school he got into, and he, unlike his friends, loved to play football - so that would be good. She also said that the high school that turned her son down only took kids in the top percent of test scores, so he might have gotten very stressed there, trying to keep up. The school that accepted him was also much more diverse, which offered a healthier, more well-rounded environment. Overall, she thought, her son would have more opportunity to shine at the school that took him. By the time we were done talking, she was absolutely relieved to see the situation in a new way - by changing her perception.

There is no competition in parenting. Your child is accomplishing her steps in life at the perfect time for her. The most important thing for your child to know is that she is okay just as she is. I believe that, in order to love ourselves, we need to know and believe without a doubt that our kids are on their perfect paths – whatever that looks like. And, we, as the moms, are the perfect mothers for our children, whatever *that* looks like. We are being guided by our intuition to the greatest and highest good for our children, and we can feel free in knowing that we are not solely responsible for where our children are.

If your child is meant to be a Michael Jordan in his/her passion - he/she will be regardless of what you put in front of him/her.

My child's path will probably be different from the norm at times, and different from his friends, and that's perfect. I hope that you can relax into the realization that sometimes experiences that initially look like road blocks are actually illuminating pathways to a beautiful new way of being. Your child's light is as bright as every other child out there –no matter what your experience is right now

Affirmations to Honor Your Child

All children have room to be magnificent in their lives.

My child is following his perfect life path. I honor it, whatever it looks like.

I honor every parent, knowing that I am just as important as every parent that exists.

I am never alone in my choices for my children. I am intuitively guided at all turns.

I listen to intuition for guidance as I let go and allow for my child to be exactly who he/she is supposed to be.

I claim oneness in all children and parents. We are all equal experiencing exactly what we are supposed to experience.

I lay down any need to prove myself or to prove my child is good enough and I rise up to knowing that we are both good enough just as we are.

My Hands Are Tied: I Am a Healer

The evening before my middle daughter's fifth birthday party, I was in great need of an uninterrupted night of sleep. Not only was my family planning to be here, we also had 13 little girls coming over and I had to be alert and ready for the big event. During this particular time of life, my kids were all coming into our room during the middle of the night - just about every night and each at different times. I had done my sage smudging and that worked for awhile. Then the middle-of-the-night wanderings into our room started up again. Needless to say, on this particular night before a big party, I was praying for a full night of sleep.

At around 1:00 a.m., I awakened to my son talking to my husband about a belly ache. Falling back asleep, I thought, "Thank goodness he woke Brian up and not me..." Then around 3:30 a.m. my son came back into our room and woke me up saying that he thought he was going to throw up. For a split second I thought, "Maybe I'll just let him run to the bathroom alone... I'm so tired. I'm sure he's fine..." Then the self-talk changed to, "My mom would have gotten up with me. I'm the mother... I need to be nurturing right now." Wandering to the bathroom, I found my son moaning and rolling around on the floor. He said he felt like there was a piece of metal in his stomach that needed to get out.

Finally, he did his deed. He threw up and said he felt "amazing". Within a couple of minutes though, he was back to rolling on the floor, begging to get this feeling out of his body. I'd seen stomach bugs like this before, and immediately a false belief came to me that I could do nothing for my son. My hands were tied. That it would be a matter of hours before everyone was throwing up. And I felt so bad for him, remembering what the flu was like for me as a kid, and even nowadays as an adult. His sister's birthday party was in just a few hours, but I'd forgotten all about it.

Then I started thinking about the fact that I am his mother, and that I could help here more than I realized. Beginning with a grace-full willingness to be in the now moment, I could take in the situation, with my son and me lying there on the bathroom floor in the middle of the night. I took in the sacredness of a mother with her son, nurturing and loving him as he felt such pain. I could recognize the gift that I got to be the one he wanted to be with in this uncomfortable experience.

In that moment I began using my "magic wand", as Marianne Williamson calls it in her book, "Everyday Grace." We each have a magic wand, which is a "focused thought". When I use my focused thought for good, it can create miracles, and when my focused thought is negative, it will create more of the same negativity. So I began to use my magic wand, focusing my thoughts on positivity.

I put my hand on his belly and moved it around in a circular motion. I imagined light pouring out of each of my fingers into his stomach. I prayed that any congestion in his stomach was removed and that the energy in his body would flow smoothly again. I saw his perfection. Cooper wasn't "sick". He was a kid who had something in his stomach that needed to be discarded. Rubbing his belly, I "grabbed" what felt like *stuck* energy and make a motion with my hand as if to throw that energy into the toilet. I didn't think about how strange this might look to someone else – although I'm sure it would!

And throughout this process, I did not feel like it was "me" doing this. I felt a healing energy was working through me in that moment with Cooper, using my innate, intuitive guidance as the mother of my child. I saw Cooper as whole, perfect and complete. There was no pity, as I knew that what was happening was supposed to happen.

Within a few minutes of this focused, intentional thought and tummy rubbing, Cooper's rolling on the floor slowed. Then, he came to a complete stop, saying to me, "Mom, I feel so much better." He was at peace. A few minutes later, my son fell asleep on the bathroom floor. I carried him to his bed and he slept through the rest of the night.

As I went back to my bed, it felt like I'd just experienced a miracle. I believe I had experienced a power that was beyond my physical self, and it had moved through me because I was a willing vessel. This was a sacred moment in my book of memories. Originally I'd thought there was nothing I could do for my son, and it was a false belief.

Moms, we are healers with magic wands, tools we use through our hands, our eyes and our hearts. With focused thought, we can create miracles in our families – we just need to *believe* we can do it! Let's believe that we are conduits for miracles, for great change in our families. With unwavering trust, we can know that our abilities are limitless. We are the only ones who put limits in our minds.

Each of us is made of the very same energy. We have access to the same creativity and drive that has made Oprah, *Oprah*. We have access to the same intelligence and wisdom that made Alexander Graham Bell capable of inventing the telephone. We have access to the same abundance that has made Warren Buffet one of the wealthiest people in the world. And we have access to the same compassion that made Mother Teresa, *Mother Teresa*. We each just need to believe it.

I hope for all moms, for you who are reading this now, that you realize just how powerful the love is that you have in your hearts. The core of who you are is love. Underneath the resistance, the resentment, the victim mentality, the shame is love. Peel it all away and love is all that is left. I pray that you realize your power, and that you arm yourselves with your "magic wands"! Let's allow life to use each of us for good. Miracles happen every day. Let's be living examples!

Affirmations to Affirm that I am a Healer

I am a powerful mother with healing energy at my fingertips.

I remove my pre-conceived ideas and make room for miracles.

I let go of my history and allow for new inspired ways of being to saturate my life.

I use my magic wands – my thoughts and words – to transform my experiences.

Underneath everything is love. I am love.

My blind spots are uplifted so that I can see all options in front of me.

I see myself through unconditionally loving eyes.

People-Pleasing: I Give and Receive in Perfect Balance

Do you have a hard time saying "no" to your family or to other people who ask for your time? When you can't quite get the "no" out, do you later find that you are upset with yourself? Does a mandatory "yes" feel like that is all the value you have to offer people, because you don't know what else you have to give?

I've learned that saying "yes" when you mean "no" is an easy way to get people to like us. We are often so focused on taking care of our families - and we really *love* to take care of our families - that we, as moms, forget that we need to be taken care of as well. We forget that we have our own needs and desires. Our choices all too often get based on what our family and our friends want and need, right? Sometimes we get lost in giving, thinking that it's selfish when we want to do something for ourselves.

I remember a phase when I was not able to pick out what to wear in the morning. I would actually ask my husband, "Should I wear this shirt or that blouse?" Lost in being a mom and saying "yes" to everyone else, I had lost myself. I had turned into a shell of myself, with what seemed to be *nothing* inside. It felt like I was only a vessel meant to pour out all I had to my family. What happened to those passions I used to have, like writing songs and poetry and playing the piano? Those pieces of my authentic self were just memories from my past, and I couldn't imagine having a moment to revive a single passion.

Being a people pleaser also mattered to me because saying "yes" to other people that needed help felt good, at least temporarily. I've also believed that people wouldn't like me if I didn't help them out, so saying "yes" was my "insurance policy" that they'd like me for at least another day. Yes, that sounds crazy! In truth, we each have so much to offer a friend. We moms just lose sight of that sometimes.

When I finally realized that I was lost in people-pleasing and taking care of others at the expense of myself, I thought, "How did this happen? I don't even know who I am anymore!" It's really no wonder that this loss of self happens to some of us. We spend most of our time doing our mothering job and our careers, which is beautiful - but who lets us know what we need to do in order to keep ourselves in balance?

A false belief says that loving moms are also selfless givers, but the truth is that we are *both* givers *and* receivers. With so much on our plates each day, we forget about that second piece sometimes. Stay-at-home moms give to their children and family each and every day. Working mothers have their careers, and then they come home and give, give, give. No wonder moms get out of balance! We *give* constantly, and when we get used to this, it becomes a pattern in our lives - and then we give more. When it's time to "receive", receiving feels uncomfortable and even selfish.

Where did this false belief come from, the one that says that what *I* need is selfish now that I'm a mom and that there is no longer any room for me to be m*e?*

To be in balance, there needs to be receiving AND giving in life.

Picture a pitcher of lemonade. You keep pouring the lemonade out until there is none left. Once the pitcher is empty, you don't keep trying to pour more lemonade. You need to make more, and fill up the pitcher again. Your life is like that pitcher. It needs to be filled up on a daily basis. Otherwise, you are giving more than you have to give, and that is not healthy for you or anyone else.

As mothers, I also think it's valuable for our children to see us as well- rounded, confident and authentic people. What is good for me is good for my whole family. Do you want your kids to see parenthood as a time when a mom loses who she is in order to do everything for everyone else? It's much more valuable for our kids to see us following our deepest heart's desires. In fact, a child needs to see his or her mother doing something that she has passion for, like exercising or taking an art class or playing the piano. You teach your children about *their* value by showing them how you see *your* value.

So, my question to you is: What do *you* need? Start small. Ask yourself, "Is there anything that I want?" Keep it simple, like choosing "I want to eat chicken tonight" rather than asking your husband or children what they want. Then, besides being with your children, what do you like to do? Maybe it's "I loved singing in my band before I had kids." Or, "I have always wanted to learn how to play the piano." These were two of mine. So, I started small. I joined up with the band at my spiritual center and sang back-ups. Pretty soon, I got to sing some lead parts. Now I write songs in my home and sing at open mic nights. In the process I've made some lifelong friends and I've honored my heart's desires.

What would make your heart sing? Because it is so important for you to *feel* alive. Starting small is actually a big step! You are honoring yourself. You are honoring your path as a parent and as a mother and as a woman when you listen to and act upon your own heart's desires.

Now there are many people who say "yes" to lots of requests and they are perfectly happy doing so. For those of us who have a difficult time saying "no" to people, we must remember that behind that hard-to-say "no" is a precious, authentic, strong, confident woman who wants to be heard. There's a passionate, independent, amazing woman who dreams of shining in her own light. Behind that "no" you want to say is the woman that everyone wants to know and *needs* to know! Your authentic "yes" or "no" is also right for everyone involved, when it is honoring you and your choice.

Looking again at your children, how do you want your children to be when they are with their friends? Don't we want our kids to be strong, authentic, independent, confident people? Face it - we want our children to say "no" when they need to. We want them to say "yes" when it feels authentically right for them. So, we can help create this reality by demonstrating it in our own lives.

I challenge you to really think about your true, authentic answers and choices before you make them. As you balance out your "yes's" and "no's", you will have more time to honor your own creative needs and desires. Say "yes" to yourself! Each time you do, being in balance will get easier and easier.

Affirmations for Giving and Receiving in Balance

I honor myself and choose what feels right to me

I respect everyone around me by walking in my truth

Speaking up about my needs gives my child a good role model.

I am a living, vibrant, passionate person. My needs are fulfilled.

Any passion that I have is fully sourced and supported by life itself.

I am an authentically charged woman who sees my path clearly. I speak the truth with everyone.

My true friends will respect and love me even when I say "no".

Playing Roles: I Express Myself as Authentically Me

For most of my life, I walked around with something out of balance that I could never put into words. It felt like I was playing roles everywhere I went. I think this began because I was a quiet kid and didn't always have the magical "right things" to say or add to a conversation. So, I became a chameleon.

I could morph into any situation I was in – always a little awkwardly though, and never quite getting it right. As I got older, this chameleon got tested. I began hanging out with some very real, authentic people, and I started experiencing anxiety and nervousness when we'd get together because my chameleon couldn't easily project a different *me* around these people. It was like I was being called to be myself – but who was that? I'd hidden behind roles my whole life! I was a banker, a marathon runner, a songwriter, a singer, a mom, and a wife…. but what did that all mean as far as having a real conversation with someone?

Being a parent amplified this insecurity. Because I didn't know who I really was, I questioned everything I did as a parent. Not only did I want to do the "right" things, I wanted to be the well dressed, put together mom who looked well rested and highly fashionable, complete with her perfectly attired children. My role as mother was more about how it looked to other people. I also was trying to make things happy and peaceful in our house, because it was good for the children. But I was burning up on the inside! I *wasn't* feeling happy and peaceful.

It was as if my chameleon was being drained of its colors. There was nowhere to hide anymore. Everyone around me was so authentic and free, and I was busy organizing my roles, trying to figure out new ones to fit in to my life. But who I was used to being was being challenged at every corner. I had a false belief that I would only fit in if I was the same as everyone else - that I didn't have a special, authentic personality underneath all of my chameleon roles.

Express yourself as authentically you.

What does the word "authentic" mean? There are two definitions that I found: *undisputed credibility* and *genuineness, or the quality of being genuine or not corrupted from the original.*

Wow. Why would I ever create roles in the first place? Well, as a teenager I didn't like who I was. Because I didn't feel secure, I created ways of being that seemed better at the time. Those ways of being then stuck with me, and my authenticity felt further and further removed from me. The result: I didn't feel credible, and I was corrupted from my original self.

The truth is that there was never anything missing in me in the first place and there's nothing missing in you. I am good enough. You are good enough. You are authentic. You are perfect and complete and you have everything you could ever need inside of you right now. You are not who you genuinely are by-accident – you were made on purpose. You are someone who doesn't need to *try* to be liked. You are liked in your authentic being. You were born with specific unique gifts which may have *never* been seen before because you judged yourself as a child and didn't allow them to show through.

What do you like to do? What are you drawn to creatively? Have you always wanted to take an art class, or to ride horses? Those passions that your chameleon insists you don't have time for - well, those are *you* – authentically! Say "yes" to them – to at least one of them! Feel the excitement of doing something that passionately fills you.

How do we move away from the chameleon, those roles that we've established as our reality? Here are the steps that I recommend:

- ♦ The first step is recognizing the chameleon. Call yourself out.

- ♦ Realize that you are authentically filled with gifts and personality that are good enough. In fact, they are amazing enough to use day to day, without playing any roles.

- Pay attention to thoughts like, "I've always wanted to do this," or, "That would be so much fun!" That's your authentic self speaking up. Listen and take action.

- Realize that you do not have to control any conversation or relationship. You are not in charge of or responsible for that. Just your being in the room is enough.

- If you feel anxiety about saying the right thing or making a funny joke, calm yourself down before you get into the situation. As you walk or drive to the event, quiet your mind. Center yourself. Relax and remind yourself that you are enough. Your anxiety is your signal that your chameleon wants to come out and take over. Walk into the room knowing that you are safe. That there are no expectations of you. You don't need to "do" or "be" anything to be liked.

- You know what is *really* not good for your kids? Faking that you are peaceful and happy, and pretending that everything is okay when sometimes it isn't. Allow your emotions and feelings to come and go in your home. Let your kids know when you are having a "bad" day and when you're not feeling happy, and let them know if it has nothing to do with them.

- You are enough in your quietness, your quirkiness, your un-coordinated-ness or whatever your "-ness" is. You are enough. Trust yourself that everything about you is important and special.

One of the first times that I felt utter peace in a situation with new people was when I went to pick my youngest child up from preschool. I used to feel like I had to say "hello" to everyone and have the perfect "nice thing to say" or a compliment to give. The moms in this group all knew each other and would be in deep conversation together when I arrived to pick up my daughter. I felt like I had to work at joining in with them. While I truly meant my compliments to these women, it also felt I was giving compliments to be accepted as a member of the group. One day I focused on my way to the preschool. I reminded myself that "I am enough" and that I needed to be quiet and present with my daughter.

Instead of making the small talk to fit in, I walked in, hugged my daughter, and walked us out to the car - feeling authentic and light and free. There was no need to impress anyone or to manipulate acceptance of myself from anyone. I accepted myself that day and do you know what is so amazing? I learned that people can sense when we aren't being authentic. Since that day at the preschool pick up, I didn't worry about how I looked or what I said, and the moms started saying hello to me.

I think when we are younger, we feel vulnerable - like any differences and unique, special qualities we have that separate us from the crowd are negative. After all, at that age we only want to be seen as part of the crowd. Now, as adults and as moms, it is our time to burst forth with these unique differences. We have gifts and talents that only we can express. Express yourself as authentically *you*!

Affirmations for Expressing Yourself Authentically

I am an authentic human being with special gifts to give myself and the world!

I am free and safe to be me. God made everyone so I am whole, perfect and complete just as I am.

I am safe in my own skin.

I am safe in every social situation I am in.

My authentic silence is sacred in a room full of people.

I let go of old beliefs that I am not good enough for other people. I raise and praise myself as who I am. People love me for who I am.

Resentment: I Walk in My Own Power

Resentment builds up when I don't talk about my needs. It bubbles up in me when I'm not happy in my life and I'm judging someone else's life as better than mine. Resentment stays with me when I don't communicate my unhappiness, or I blame someone else for my unhappiness.

When we're first dating, and when we're newly married, many of us tend to brush off inconveniences and potential relationship issues rather easily, just because we're so happy to be with our partner. That's the honeymoon phase, right? But, after some years - *and* some children - those things that we could brush off before have become less easy to sweep under the rug.

I have heard this basic story many times when it comes to resentment in a couple's relationship. This example is from a family where the mom stayed home with her kids and her husband had a career outside the house. When I speak with the wife, she tends to talk about how unappreciative her husband is, saying things like, "He gets to go out to lunch every day on his own -at a restaurant! I've been eating PB&Js this week, *if* I get to eat anything!" Or, "He refuses to help me at home because he says it's *my* job – he says his job is to bring home a paycheck."

Then I hear his side. "So, she goes to play dates all day while I'm bustin' my butt at work trying to keep this family afloat, and she's complaining that I'm not helping with bath time!" and "I've got a lot of stress on me to support this family and she's off chatting with her friends while the kids play in the basement."

It has become him against her, and it's easy to see that there is a lot of resentment on *both* sides. This resentment comes from a "someone has to win" environment, where each person has to win at being the hardest worker. Neither of them feels safe to help the other person because if they do, they fear this "help" will somehow be used against them. For the wife, it goes like this, "If I say he's doing a great job I'm afraid he'll

84

think he's won and that he'll think I'm admitting that his job is harder than mine and he won't help me at all." This is a conversation I've had numerous times with many married friends who are parents. Usually each parent feels that she or he is doing more than the other and rather than talking about it, their feelings are most commonly expressed through passive-aggressive action.

A mom who has resentment can also be covering up the feeling of being left behind. She is in a false belief that says she has no control over her day-to-day experience. She believes that she's a victim of her circumstances and feels unappreciated. She thinks her words are not heard or valued. Often she finds herself in another false belief that tells her that her personal good comes from the outside world – not from inside of her. A mom who is feeling resentment like this has started putting more power in what is happening around her, like she is sitting in the back seat of the car. She has forgotten that she is actually in the driver's seat of her own power, of her life.

Walk in your power as your authentic self.

Moms, we get to decide how our life is going to be and how our day will unfold. We get to decide if we are going to continue this competition with our spouse or if we are going to use our voice to speak our truth so that this resentment can end. We get to say No and Yes, and we get to use our voice for choosing the best options in our life. We get to appreciate ourselves, so that we can then shore up the energy of appreciation and receive it from others. We get to walk in our own POWER – to walk in the fulfillment of our dreams and our hopes for our relationship. If I want more appreciation, then I need to appreciate myself and everything around me. I need to walk in the fulfillment of what I want. I project my power, my self-love, and my confidence, and I attract it right back to me.

Can I be the one to take the first step towards peace in whatever my situation is? If it's a competition with my spouse, can I be the *first* person to speak up in my power? When I feel resentment, it's something inside of me that is signaling me that I need to go deeper and I need to speak my truth. What is it that I am not appreciating in myself? What am I not happy about in my life? What is it that I'm not appreciating in my spouse, or my friend, or my child? How have I given away my power?

It's so important not to ignore your resentment. It is coming up for a purpose – it's a signal. You can then use your resentment as a signal that something out of balance in your life. Ask yourself: How have I forgotten to speak from my power? What experiences are happening now because I didn't speak my true authentic voice? Then, you can move from resenting silently to speaking up powerfully, and from self-love. I know it can feel scary to speak your truth. When you do it though, you will feel empowerment and freedom! If you feel like speaking your truth is impossibly difficult, think of a famous actress or someone that you know that speaks up from empowerment, and pretend that you are her. I absolutely promise - you will feel the weight of resentment fall off of your back.

In the chapter on Anger, we talked about anger as a seed in our consciousness. Sometimes anger can flare up, and when we see this happening, then we can love the anger and calm it back down again to its seed state. It is the same for resentment – or any other emotion that you have that you don't feel good about. If you are always feeling resentful, your resentment seed has been watered a lot – in fact it has probably had a torrential downpour on that seed for a long time, and turned into a full-fledged garden! You've focused your attention on it with some gusto, and now the resentment feels like it will never go away.

Well, we need to start watering the other seeds in our consciousness – the love seed, the joy seed, and the gratitude seed. What you put your attention on is what will manifest in your life. The less attention you give your resentment, the less it will come up for you. I challenge you to speak your truth today! You are worth it! Whatever it is that you are holding against someone else, it is only hurting you. Walk in your own power instead and speak your truth.

Affirmations to Walk in Your Own Power

I am so grateful for my life.

I am so grateful for any support that I have.

I am so grateful for my children.

When I show up in gratitude, more of the good shows up in my life.

I pay more attention to what my spouse does for me then what he doesn't do.

I speak my needs as I need them. This brings me closer to my authentic self.

I pay more attention to my life and my accomplishments than my shortcomings.

If I need something from someone I ask for it and I claim celebration for speaking up.

I value my relationship with my spouse enough to honor our communication and my needs.

I create boundaries in my life so that my needs are always fulfilled.

Resistance: I Surrender to Allowing

I'm at a ballet class for my second child and she's four years old. She is clinging to my leg again, as she has every week since the first class. During the first class she was totally fine - excited and having a blast. Now, for some reason she just clings to me. I see all of the other kids running in and hugging the teacher. But here, clinging to me as if she will wilt away if I let go, is my daughter.

The same happened when they got older, whether it was committing to a recital and then refusing to go out of fear, or refusing to go to a birthday party that they said "yes" to.

And it's not the first time this has happened. Something like this has happened with each of my kids. As I write this, my youngest daughter, who has been in a gymnastics class for two whole terms with no issues, will now not let go of me during her class either, and I'm actually *in* the class with her! She holds on so tight it's like she's afraid of everything around her.

How does this make me feel? Honestly, I feel resistance. I feel anger sometimes, and frustration. It happens over and over again and to be real, I'm a little tired of it. Why can't my kids be the ones that go fearlessly into class? What am I doing wrong that causes this to happen? I get in a space where I am certain something is wrong, and all I feel is resistance.

Another trigger for me is when I am running late – and I hate to be late! It's morning and I've asked the kids to get their coats on three times - and nobody is listening. As the stress level rises, my voice starts to get louder. "Come on, we are going to be late for school! If you had been listening in the first place, we wouldn't be running late!" I notice that my kids are getting slower and slower as I'm getting more and more anxious.

When things don't go the way I want them to, this inner resistance is all about wanting my control back. Things are supposed to go my way, and they aren't. This can make me even feel disrespected at times. And, at the very root of this need for control of my environment is fear. When I'm resisting my life, I'm afraid that something else or someone else is in control, and it doesn't feel okay. I don't feel safe.

Resistance like this carries a false belief that tells me I'm not okay when things don't go the way I expect them to. This false belief warns me that I'm only safe when I'm in control and things go my way. Oddly enough, the only *real* "security blanket" is the freedom to allow life to happen. I allow myself to be free from any resistance by releasing my preconceived ideas and accepting whatever life looks like in that moment.

Surrender and be in the space of allowing.

When our kids don't do what we want them to do, we often feel a tug, a pull that *our* way is the way it has to be. Like, when you've called it a night and the kids want to take their time getting into bed. You know, there are just those things they want to see or do before they say goodnight. When I'm tired, I want time to myself. If it's been a long day, the only thing I want is to crawl into my own bed. And some nights we moms can see the mess that still needs cleaning up after the kids are in bed. Are there some limits to be set with the kids? Sure. And, sometimes we have trouble accepting what is happening in the Now. We resist, instead of simply allowing the bedtime pace to be what it is.

Parents can also resist a child's learning patterns, like when we're helping our children with homework. My son gets very stressed out when he's doing his homework, and when I help him I can feel resistance filling me because I think homework is no big deal. Or, I get impatient because I've explained something to him and he's not listening. Other parents have shared with me that their kids can get really worked up when they do homework together. We have to accept what is, and surrender to allowing our children to do their homework in a way that works best for them – even if we want it to look different.

89

My children are my teachers. They show me that, even when things don't go the way I'd planned, they go exactly as they are supposed to go. When I resist this life lesson, I'm passing up a chance for real growth. But, you and I can also rely on the fact that another chance to learn will come.

How can we release this urge to resist? As soon as you realize that you're running late, be willing to accept that you are supposed to be running late. If your child doesn't want to eat, let it go. Resistance won't help the situation. Resisting the fact that my child clearly doesn't want to go into her ballet class not only puts stress on me and on her, it probably stresses the people around us. My own goal as a mother is to be in the space of allowing. There's so much freedom even just saying that word: *allowing*.

I mentioned how important it is for me to be on time. When I release my need to control time, I can allow my life to happen at the speed it is supposed to happen. If I can trust that my life is in "the right time", all of the time – not just when the clock says I'm "on time" - I can relax into every situation with my children.

Clearly, there are times when we really need to be on time, like when you need to get to work or to an appointment. This isn't about being "la-dee-da" about time commitments. When you begin accepting your life and allowing for it to flow, you will be more aware of opportunities that will honor your ability to be on time. You'll be in a place of seeing things more clearly so that natural consequences can happen. Perhaps it's about beginning a little earlier in the morning, or even allowing your child to go to school in his pajamas.

Here's what I've discovered to be true: The more you can allow what is happening in your life, the less your child will act up. He won't have any "buttons" of yours to push because you've cleared out all of that resistance. Your children can see that they don't get under your skin. And when you accept and allow what is happening, your children will follow suit.

Affirmations to Surrender To Allowing

Life happens through me, not to me.

I accept everything today that happens exactly as it does.

I allow for life to flow today, removing any preconceived ideas of how I want it to look.

I let go and let life happen.

I release any need to control my child and I relax into his own divine timing.

What I resist will persist, so I open myself to learning how to release my fear-based desire to control.

I accept my child for exactly who she is. I honor her and her needs knowing she is exactly where she is supposed to be.

Self-Deprecation: I Accept and Appreciate Myself
When we moms are in self-deprecation mode, we find ourselves swimming in a pool of thoughts like, "I'm not enough... I am not a good parent... I should have done this ... I shouldn't have said that ... I'm not active enough...I'm not fun to be with...I'm not creative ... I'm too tired", and on and on. No wonder I don't feel good sometimes, with a voice coming from me like that – who would? In moments like this we're covering up the truth of who we are: a person that is just has important and interesting as the most important and interesting person you know!

We not only do this to ourselves but I know many of us cut ourselves down every single day.

These "I'm not enough" thoughts are rooted in a false belief that tells me there's something wrong with me, when in the big picture of life there's nothing wrong with me. I'm growing at my own pace learning what I am supposed to be learning. I like to look at being here living this life as a classroom. We all have our own lessons that we need to learn and our own ways to grow. And I believe that the ultimate goal in life is complete unconditional love for everything and everyone – most importantly, ourselves.

Sometimes we criticize ourselves because we are honestly trying to be humble. Other times aren't so well-purposed. There have been times when someone has told me that he thinks my child is well-behaved. I've responded, "Oh gosh, I'm lucky today. You should see him at home!" Other times a friend has commented that I cooked a great dinner, and my reply was, "My poor family has had to deal with my horrible cooking for years!" Have you had similar experiences? You take a compliment and try to even it out somehow by bringing yourself down again. Unfortunately, this "humility" has nothing to do with being humble. It is hurtful, because you are not accepting a compliment to enter your life. You are not allowing yourself to *receive*. You are not accepting *you*.

You deserve to feel appreciated and accepted for who you are at all times.

When I downplay a sincere compliment, I am not accepting my true nature. I'm probably a person who isn't fully comfortable with being seen, especially being seen as something wonderful! But today, when someone gives me a compliment, I work at saying, "Thank you!" I don't describe how I got the shirt on sale or how I just got back from getting a haircut that I'll never be able to style on my own. I stop and say, "Thank you." And then I zip it. Give it a try. You are worth it!

When we apologize for how we handle our children - I've heard a mom say, "I know it's probably overboard to not let my child eat sugar" or "I know I'm over the top to stick so tightly to my child's schedule", we negate our intuitive choices for our children rather than standing up for them. I think we parents need to be proud of our choices and not apologize for them. Stand strong for what you believe in, and you might even inspire others with your self-confidence.

As a mom, I know there can be so much pressure on us. There's the pressure that we put on ourselves, the pressure that we feel other people put on us, and strong judgments of which way is "right" and which way is "wrong". Moms want to do everything *perfectly* for our children, and we believe that there is no room for mistakes. This energy can slowly eat away at our sense of worthiness. Some time passes, and the next thing we know, we don't even like ourselves much anymore. Who is the first person to tell you when you are doing something that's wrong? You! It's your inner voice that lets you know when you're always falling short or that "you are so stupid". That's the voice that would be jailed if it was visible in the human world.

What does the voice inside your head say to you about who you are? If you are anything like me, the voice inside my head used to be an over-bearing disciplinarian that only accepted perfection – and usually perfection wasn't even quite right. I would beat myself up over even minor things. The voice that I now listen to, which I call the divine mother, is the voice that only expresses love for me. This awareness about self-love came to me about a year ago, when I was in a place of wondering why I wasn't feeling very good about myself. I was meditating, being in the now moment, and doing everything that I thought would help me, but it wasn't working. Then I focused in on my "self-talker", and it was not a pretty experience.

When I compared that "self –talker" in my head to a parent, I discovered an inner voice that was a bully, nasty, controlling, and non-accepting. No wonder I didn't feel worthy to parent! Who *could*? You see, we really can't hide any aspect of ourselves. We can't act like we have it all together, and then, when we are alone, criticize everything that we did that day - not if we want true peace. How could anyone be a well-rounded, loving mother with an abusive, inner "self-talker" that didn't like anything she did?

I've also learned that this rigid voice in my head is who shows up and parents my children when I am in a highly stressed-out moment. Through meditation and affirmations, I practice transforming my stern, abusive "internal parent" into loving and nurturing voice. And that sweet, supportive voice in my head (and in your head) is actually *unconditional love.*

For me, the change came in an instant. I felt acceptance and relief. Now, throughout each day, this transformed "self-talker" tells me what a great job I'm doing. She nurtures me when I'm feeling stressed. She loves me when I feel tired or angry or judged. The other critical voice no longer bombards me with negativity, but I do need to remind myself, sometimes daily, of my loving, accepting "self-talker". The more I practice, the easier it gets. And this has affected my parenting, softening me so that I am *accepting* of my children just the way they are.

There is a light inside of you that is authentic to you. This light burns as brightly as the sun. You may feel in a fog occasionally and even in the dark at times, but the reality is that the sun is always shining no matter what you are experiencing– and that is truth. Each of us is important, simply because we are here. We can love ourselves as we love our children – unconditionally, all of the time.

Affirmations to Accept and Appreciate Yourself

I am the perfect parent for my child.

My child chose me to be his parent. I honor him for that.

Underneath that tiny exterior known as my child is a complete and fully-matured spirit that has all of the answers. I just need to look deeper in myself to see this in my child.

I am filled with the light energy of life. It radiates from me and brightens every step I take.

A Mother's Manual for Self-Love

I am one with life. I was made with specific purpose.

I honor ME today! I shine brightly with no apologies.

I let go of any judgment of myself and I acknowledge my inner Divine Mother. I allow her to parent me today.

I accept myself just as I am, and I feel a love for myself that I inspire my children to feel about themselves.

Shame: I Come from Unconditional Love

Where does shame show up for you? Has someone ever embarrassed you for something that you did? Has anyone ever singled you out and tried to make you feel wrong or bad in front of other people? Have you ever felt ashamed of something about yourself, something you hide and don't want anyone to know about? Do you feel ashamed of choices that you've made in life? My guess is that most of us can answer "yes" to each of these questions. For me, I can now see that I felt deserving of shame, and kept drawing those types of situations to myself.

Before I was married, I had an experience with a former boyfriend that made me feel completely ashamed and embarrassed. He and I were shopping for a new watch for him, and we were planning to use two different jewelry stores to find the best price. As we arrived in the second store and were talking with the jeweler, I told the jeweler the price that was quoted to us from the first store, thinking that this man might give us a lower price. Instantly, I felt my boyfriend's eyes burning through me. He turned and walked out of the store, walking about 10 feet in front of me and unwilling to talk to me or tell me what made him so angry. I didn't know what to say or do!

We got into his car to meet some of his friends for a drink, with him driving all the way there in angry, stony silence. Once we got to the bar, he still refused to even look at me. As he told his friends the story, they all laughed at me for ruining his chances at a better deal by disclosing the price to soon. The next day, and with me sitting there, he told his family about what happened. I felt so stupid – and I didn't really even know what I'd done wrong. I felt ashamed, small and completely deflated.

Now fast forward to many years later, and two weeks in a row where I had no time away from my children. I'm feeling at the end of my rope. Unconsciously I take that experience from my past and realize how it worked in its own negative way, and I shame my child because I need to feel in control again.

Most of us experienced shame at some point in our lives. Chances are those memories still live in you, and there is some healing that can happen for you. Reveal the truth of who you are, the truth that you are whole, perfect and complete, just as you are. The false belief that tells us that being shamed or feeling shame means there is something wrong with us is *false*.

Everything that you are is beautiful and perfect, no matter what that looks like.

The truth is that if you feel ashamed about something it's you believing you need to be perfect. If a person has "shamed" you in your past, it's important to understand that the person involved was most likely feeling insecure and out of control. For my old boyfriend, shaming me was an easy way out for him, and it came from his space of fear. There is nothing true about any shame that you or I felt in our past. It's the result of the work of another person who lost control and needed it back and didn't know a healthy way to do it.

I have felt ashamed of ways that I've behaved in my past. For example, some of the choices I made when I was in college and in my early 20s, I felt and still sometimes feel a bit of shame looking back at who I was and shame for making choices that were not good for anyone including me. When we feel shame because of ways we've behaved that we aren't proud of, it's ok to use that shame as a sign to shift our behaviors. Most importantly though, move up and on from it. There is no need to keep replaying it over and over. Get the lesson and move on.

If you have felt shame in your past, and you have not dealt with it and taken the power out of it, there is a chance you might use "shaming" techniques in your parenting, especially when you handle a situation from an unconscious place. For example, something that I've heard myself say to my child in an unconscious moment is, "Oh my gosh, of course you left your mess out – you act like you are three years old!" Or, maybe you have heard other parents say, "Bad boy!" or "That was so stupid of you to do".

Sometimes it's more the tone of what we are saying than the words we choose. When I am at the end of my tether and don't feel that inner peace anymore, I become unconscious and speak from an unconscious place. I'm not thinking about my words – and I will most likely use whatever quick and easy style of "feeling better" that works for me. If that shame-based style worked on me, I unconsciously believe it can work on my children.

But, there is no separation between my children and me. When I am using shame, I am looking for power in what I feel is a powerless situation. I am trying to feel "better than" or "bigger than". I believe that when we shame our children, we are acting out from past experiences, speaking without awareness. We are simply re-enacting something from our past. When I bring awareness to myself today – awareness of my intention for my words to my child - I can see my true intention before I speak. If my primary intention is to make my child feel bad or less-than, or for me to feel power, I work on shifting my presence to the now-moment and shifting my words.

Sometimes I might walk away for a moment to breathe, so that I don't say something I'll regret. Then, as I take a deep breath, I say to myself, "I love you! You aren't alone... (*Breathe!*) Be calm, you are okay (*Breathe!*)" The more proactive I can be, the better I handle the situation. There are healthy, logical, non-emotional ways of showing consequences when a child acts out. Shaming my child will hurt me, my child, and our relationship - now, and in the long run.

Think of a time when you felt ashamed. How did it feel? Think about how old you were and who was there dishing out the shame. Bring yourself to that moment, and see how you looked and how you felt. Go there as much as you are able and really feel what you felt. I want you to give that younger version of you a big hug and say, "I love you – you are perfect just as you are.

Release yourself from any sense of deserving this. You are going to be okay."

Send love to that younger person that you were. Allow that love to permeate through you. You are deserving of unconditional love and support. I know that you can give this unconditional love and support to your own children too. As you learn to love yourself and accept yourself, you will notice that you are more accepting of your children. Try out the self-love lessons in the back of this book. As you learn to accept yourself and love yourself, you will find that you will automatically parent differently because you aren't afraid anymore. You will feel safe. If you find yourself having trouble shifting away from shame in your parenting style, ask for guidance. Go within, or go to a friend. The answers are inside of you; you just need to ask. So, do the work, you are worth it! And so are your children.

Affirmations for Giving Yourself Unconditional Love

I come from unconditional love whenever I speak to my children

I am whole – I am complete – I am alive, awake and aware. I am fully funded by Spirit!

I use the power from Spirit to discipline my children.

Even if I don't feel it, I am always sourced by my intuition.

When I discipline, I build my child's confidence by showing up as a loving guide for him.

My voice is full of unconditional love. Love leads every word I say.

I love and accept myself for who I am.

I release any belief that I deserved to feel shame in my younger life.

I crack open a new way of talking to my kids from love!

Things Will Never Change: I Trust That A New Moment is Always Coming

Two months into my third child's aggressive acid reflux, I was moaning, "When is this going to end?" I had to give Violet some medicine a half hour before she could eat her meals, and then she needed to be held upright for 45 minutes after she ate. That meant that if she was up at 4:00 a.m., I had to walk around with a crying, hungry baby for 30 minutes before she could eat. Then, when I could finally feed her, there was that "hold her upright for 45 minutes after a meal" to look forward to. Violet slept on a wedge-shaped pillow because she couldn't lie flat. We joked that she was like a human bottle of soda: if you tilted her, everything came out. This daughter of mine didn't lie flat on her back until she was seven months old!

Of course, I was exhausted and heartbroken for Violet as this ritual became my reality day in and day out for months. My other two children also needed attention, love and support. After several months, I remember laying Violet flat in her crib for the first time and feeling scared. And then, she grew out of it and I could treat her normally. As life moved on and got easier, I realized that everything changes – even what seems unbearable at the time.

When I started believing that the current reality would never change, I was in a false belief that told me that I am forgotten, that I am stuck, and that I have no control over my life or my thoughts. The truth is that *everything* evolves. And it's true; we often don't have control over things that happen in our lives. What we *can* do though is find things to support and nurture our family and ourselves.

Have faith because life is always changing, and we all shift and change right along with life.

On March 6, 2010 I woke up with a dizzy spell. I've had dizzy spells throughout my life so I knew that usually a good night of sleep cures it. By the first evening though, I was spinning in every direction. I couldn't function so I went to bed hoping I'd feel better in the morning. Some days went by that I could function but usually by early evening I had to be in bed. After about two weeks of this, things shifted for the worse, and I couldn't get out of bed. I couldn't open my eyes and I felt like everything had to be silent. My parents came in to town to help take care of me because my husband was in the middle of trying to change careers, and move us to a new town. After an MRI, an emergency room visit and visits to a neurologist, and finally a move to my parent's house for a week, I started to get better. My mom said to me, "every second all the parts of your body are working together to make you better." For me, I believe that is what healed me. Because I felt stuck – completely stuck in my situation of my dark quiet bedroom. I didn't think anything would change, day after day after day of complete dizziness. I remember thinking when my kids would come into my bedroom, "If I'm dying (because at that point I didn't know that I would feel better), I can't even pretend to feel better for my kids" I bring this story up because in the midst of this hell I was in, I absolutely wondered if I would ever feel better.

I like to remind myself that no matter how much I feel that I'm struggling, there will always be a new moment. There is a light in the current experience. It's easier to see this some days more than others, but it is always there. I have to believe this, especially when I'm in a challenging situation and I don't know how long it will last. My child and I will have relief. Just knowing this can get me through anything.

I also really believe that when my child is going through a phase that is hard to understand - or maybe I have some judgment about it because it doesn't look positive - that it is a *sacred* time in my child's life, whether it is a personality issue or a physical issue, whatever it looks like. The current phase will add value to his life later on. Because I know that my child is innately good, what he is going through is simply a growth spurt that is teaching him in the most perfect way for his life. I picture him as a puzzle. For a while, all of the pieces fit together perfectly. Then there is a growth spurt that rattles the puzzle, shaking my child to the core of his being. This growth starts in a part of his brain. Then there is growth in his emotional being. Then his legs grow a bit. And for awhile everything seems off-kilter.

I work at keeping my judgment out of this process. Children can't control how they grow or whether they are in balance or not. So, I work at accepting my child's path exactly as it is, and at trusting my parenting abilities. I affirm and love every aspect of myself so I can then accept and love every aspect of my child. We mothers might want to blame ourselves or others for something our child is going through. But how can we foresee how and when our child will grow? No wonder we find our kids truly unexplainable at times! Their entire beings are growing and expanding, here and there and everywhere.

I remember a time when it was very early in the morning and I was up with Violet. I'd just given her the medicine and was holding her upright, looking out the window as I waited to feed her. I felt very present in that moment - and the moment felt heavy to me. It had been night after night of this routine for a few months and I had no idea how much longer this would be necessary. In that moment, I imagined that I was floating high up above my house, seeing the "bigger picture". I could see this moment in our lives when it was in the past. I could see Violet as a kindergartener, knowing that she's now sleeping and eating normally. I pictured her as a teenager, knowing she won't need her medicine in the wee hours of the morning anymore. I knew this present experience - with all its pain and worry - would pass.

I still use this technique when life seems lost in a dark time that will never change. Try it for yourself! Whatever your circumstance, allow your imagination to pull you out of the moment to see the bigger picture. Just knowing that change will come will make it easier to be back in the present moment. Of course, there are going to be times when you feel so thankful for everything in your life and you don't want anything to change! We also know that change is a part of life. How can we create more of these moments? The answer is *gratitude*. When I feel and express gratitude, I am actively calling to my life other things to feel grateful for. When I nurture these good moments and feel thankful for them, I can actually bring this feeling-nature into more of my day and into more of my experiences. Change your thinking, change your life. Focus on gratitude, get more gratitude!

There are moments when I feel so happy about my life. I close my eyes, if even for a breath, and I allow myself to feel grateful. I try and make the feeling I'm having *palpable*, connecting to it throughout the day. As we actively express gratitude in our lives, gifts are easier to see. This practice also helps us during times that don't feel so easy. So, let's remind ourselves that difficult moments will pass. Change will come – change towards more good, more joy and more love. We walk in the fulfillment of change for the better.

Affirmations for Trusting that a New Moment is Coming

I am in a constantly changing and flowing life pattern. I affirm that freedom is my divine nature.

I am always held in unconditional love.

I am in the now moment, knowing that this too shall pass.

My authentic nature is joy, freedom, passion and creativity. I open myself to my true nature now!

I know that my child is on his perfect, sacred path, whatever it looks like. I accept it and let it be.

What is happening right now in my life has a sacred purpose. I release and surrender and let it be.

Unhealthy Boundaries: I See Myself as Valuable and Worthy

So, we become parents – a job that we've never done before – and we are expected to figure everything out on our own, without a real handbook. "Every other parent in the world has done this, so why will it be hard for me?" I remember thinking, "am I supposed to spend all of my home time with my child? How much time is the right amount of time? We have all sorts of new relationships entering our lives and we aren't sure how to balance those. Then, we believe that we can do everything because that's what we see everybody else doing. We don't want our kids to miss out on anything so we say "yes". Sometimes we might say, "yes" to our kids because maybe we feel bad about something we said or did earlier in the day. We say "yes" to other parents and family obligations because *that's what moms do*. And we don't realize at the time what we are creating: unhealthy boundaries.

Unhealthy boundaries for me are a sign of a false belief that I get my value from giving everything that I have to everyone else. That "good moms" can do it all. We give our whole selves to everyone we meet. We give our whole selves to our children, to our work, to everyone around us. We've seen other moms sacrifice to be good. The word, "sacrifice" goes hand in hand with mothering. Over time I learned the opposite is true. When I have healthy boundaries, my life is balanced and I get my value by giving what feels good and balanced for me. I also see that not everything and not everyone will be good for me or my family. Healthy boundaries will create balance with everything in my life.

Value yourself by setting boundaries that give you balance and serenity.

My first boundary that needed to shift was with my first child. I wanted to be with him all of the time I was home. When I look back, I can see that he really became my identity. I didn't have anything else going on in my life besides my child. This can be a common occurrence with us moms, even moms that work out of the house and especially as first time parents. We tend to wrap our lives up into our child. And then, when I had my second child, it became too much for me. I was wrapped up in both of their lives and I had nothing left of my own.

This is when I started to realize that I needed to maintain my own life in order to be a healthy mother. I was so intertwined in my children's lives that I forgot that I existed as a separate person. The shift began with taking a Pilates class, which got me back into my body and gave me an hour to myself. The process takes baby steps, but this class was my first step in learning that I needed to have boundaries around living my life as an individual person.

A few years later, my new boundaries were about honestly and authentically saying "yes" and "no". I found myself saying "yes" to people just because I was trying to look like a laidback mom that had it all together. That was a tough act to perform day after day! I wasn't honoring myself because I wasn't being authentic. I was afraid to say no because I felt so accepted when I said "yes". Again, I took small steps to shift this, starting by saying "no" to a mom who needed me to watch her child on work days when the kids had off from school. Saying "no" felt so good, and ultimately the other mom found a solution that worked for her. I learned that while that first "no" is the hardest, it leads to setting more healthy boundaries.

One of the key messages through this process has been that what is authentically right for me is authentically right for everyone involved. What is authentically a "no" for me is also *right* for every person involved, no matter what the outcome looks like. If you really want to say "no", there is an authentic "yes" for the other person to discover somewhere else.

Here is a little story to demonstrate this concept. A boy asked his yellow crayon to draw a blue ocean. The yellow crayon, who felt obligated to say "yes" all of the time, said, "OK, I'll do that." Now, can the yellow crayon really color anything blue? No! It can't make a blue ocean. Eventually the yellow crayon will feel resentful and the boy will be upset. But, what can the boy do *now*? Look for the blue crayon! This whole scenario could have been avoided if the yellow crayon had just said "no". So, when you say, "yes" to something that is actually an authentic "no", you are not showing up in an authentic way as your "true "color".

Another boundary that I work on concerns access to *me*. Just because I'm home doesn't mean I can pick up the phone whenever it rings. Although I would love to have a fun conversation with a friend, if I am in the middle of something, I can set a boundary that allows me to finish what I'm doing before I have that conversation. If I am on the phone, I can teach my children to respect that time as "mommy adult time" too. I let my kids know I'm getting on the phone, and that it is respectful of them to allow for me to talk on the phone awhile without interruptions. My kids are gaining a new awareness that mom's time is valuable.

As the parent, I am also the CEO of my home, and boundaries exist around that role. If a contractor comes in and I don't feel comfortable or happy with their work, it is my job as CEO to handle it. This is about having the power to surround myself with people that are "for" me and my "company" (my family). A good corporation is successful because it attracts the right people to help run it. It also lets people go that aren't in line with the company's mission statement. It is my job to handle my home the way a Fortune 500 CEO would manage her company, so I create boundaries to keep my household running smoothly.

And then there's "me time". Whether you have a career outside or in the home, we all need to have our own time. I know how it can be for a mom when all her time, at home or outside of work, has been with her children for several days in a row. It is important to give yourself permission for your *own* time so you can remain in harmony with your self – even if the "me time" is just sitting in your living room with a nice candle burning while the kids are napping or off playing in a different room. Having date nights or girlfriend nights will feed your spirit and in turn, create healthier boundaries that make you a calmer more balanced mother. You can make sacred time for yourself, reminding you of your own uniqueness, importance, beauty and value.

Affirmations to Honor Your Boundaries

I honor my children and myself when I make boundaries.

I am healthy and vital when I live with healthy boundaries.

Boundaries are not selfish. They serve each person involved, especially me.

I allow for sacred moments throughout my day, to honor and remember my existence.

I teach my children how to live *their* lives by living a life of balance and harmony.

Boundaries allow for a safe place for our children to feel free.

I teach my children respect for ME when I honor my boundaries.

Worry: I Trust in the Flow

When two of my children clung to me in their first few weeks of school, I worried. Each child had the same experience – the teachers needed to peel them off of me while they were kicking and screaming. I felt like a bad mom leaving them this way, worried that I was ruining their confidence or that they just weren't ready to be separated from me. I worried about their emotional health, especially after it took one of my kids nearly a whole year to stop clinging.

Of course, I worried that my children would be mad at me when I picked them up from school, and that the experience would affect them as they grew older. My imagination saw their future rebellious years, when they would surely hate me because of this early childhood memory. I hung onto this worry in the beginning, talking about it with my friends, sending e-mails to family members, and getting it off my chest by discussing it in detail with my husband when he came home from work.

My days were steeped in worry. And later, as I worried about whether my children were making friends or whether they were being good friends, or would they get home okay, or if their grades would be high enough, or if they felt good about themselves and their lives, I found myself worrying that I wasn't worrying enough! After all, mothers can buy into that superstitious false belief that if we don't worry and something happens, than we are to blame, because we didn't worry enough!

When I am in worry, I am covering up the flow of trust and freedom, and I'm clearly not having faith that my intuition will guide me. *I am enveloped in a false belief that "worry means love". But, worry doesn't mean love.* My children are much better served when they know that I trust and believe in *them* – whatever the circumstance.

When I worry, the message communicated to my child is that I don't trust him/her or his/her choices – and that he can't be trusted to live his life on his own. I may even be sending him a signal that he is somehow less-than, and that I don't see him as a capable, whole, complete human being. It's as if I send out an insecurity-energy that my child can tap into.

Worry can also be a sign that I'm not trusting in myself as a parent. I have even felt more prepared when I've contemplated every possible, terrible outcome in a situation – the "what ifs". During all of this worrying, I was living in the future. I was short-tempered, and bound-up and reactive – I certainly was not acting freely. The false belief that worry equals love tells us that we have to be prepared for the worst so that we're not blindsided. It breeds an energy that tells me, as a mother, that I am not equipped or knowledgeable enough to make decisions for my family. Talk about generating some sleepless nights! Ironically - all that worry creates no positive change in the outcome of my children's lives. Instead, my children experience the same feelings of worry that I do.

Worry has no real power whatsoever, except for the power that we give it.

My daughter once went into the hospital for a simple outpatient procedure. While we were there we got to meet a little boy who was three years old. He was running around, playing, smiling, and talking to everybody. I met his mother and found out the little boy was going in for brain surgery. She told me that he'd be in a coma for at least a week, and then there would be months and months of recovery time. As our kids went in for their respective procedures, I imagined this woman's experience of that morning, and how she must have been anticipating her child's surgery over the past few weeks. I was trying to sense how she was feeling at that moment, handing her child's health and welfare over to the care of the doctors. All I could do was sit near her and know that the hands of God were guiding the doctors' hands. I could know that the hands of God would be helping her son through his recovery, and that the hands of God would be supporting her through this whole process. I saw her tears and sadness, and sent love to her. I needed to be a light beam in her consciousness so that she could know that there *is* light.

There are times when we will worry, and we need to allow ourselves to be right where we are – especially when something is happening with our child that is outside of the "norm" of every day life. The difference, though, will be that we can be aware of the worry, and be free from feeling that the worry has anything to do with the outcome of our child's experience. Living on the other side of that obsessive worry is freedom! I challenge you to practice being in the present moment if you are a frequent worrier. When you can be totally present to the moment in front of you, you will see that nothing is happening in that moment. You have inner wisdom that will guide you when you are present to it.

My experience is that worry is never intuition. Sometimes it's hard to tell and you might want to project about the future and ask yourself, "Well, what if this worry is my intuition letting me know that something is going to happen?" When we are in the now present moment, we are available to the guidance that we need. One of the biggest gifts you can give your child is to trust in his life experience and to trust in yours.

You are the most perfect mother for your child. You truly are! I pray for you to trust in that! Trust that you will know what you need to know, when you need to know it. Trust that intuition does not show up in obsessive worry. Obsessive worrying is a pattern of thinking that simply takes hold and happens without you even realizing it. Take hold of it, Moms. I am certain that you can. Check out the Love Lesson in the back of the book called "Worry Journal" to help guide you in the process.

Let's practice living beyond the belief that worry somehow keeps us prepared. Let's practice living from trust and with an open ear to guidance. *Trust yourself.*

Affirmations to Build Trust in the Now

I am in the flow of trust and freedom at all times.

I trust that intuition guides me in every moment.

I have faith that my children are on their divine, right and perfect path, whatever that looks like.

I look to the Divine Mother for guidance when I feel concern for my child. I let go and let life happen exactly as it should.

There is no mistake, only life unfolding for a greater expression of God.

I know that my child has a perfect path, and he is not just getting love from me, he is getting love from God within.

I trust in the unfolding my child's life. I trust that his life is happening perfectly for his growth.

Lessons to Support You

Finding Peace through Forgiveness

You are not defined by your past. You are only defined by how you live today.

When you look up the word 'forgiveness' in a dictionary, you will find that it means things like to grant pardon for an offense or a debt, to release any claim on an obligation or debt owed to you, to relinquish resentment against any person – including yourself.

In order to be totally present to the now-moment, it's essential to forgive ourselves for our past actions, and to forgive others for their actions against us. When we hold onto the past, we weight ourselves down with those memories. And then we make decisions - often parenting decisions- based on those old memories, which keeps them alive in us. When we forgive our past, we are free. We more easily make decisions from the now-moment, rather than from resentment, guilt, shame, entitlement or fear.

How can we let go of those memories that make us feel guilty and deserving of punishment? How do we release memories that make us feel anger and resentment towards someone else? One word – *forgiveness*. There are experiences from my own past that I've felt guilty about. Whenever I've thought about them, these experiences have also felt like they just happened moments ago, when in truth it was actually years ago! I've learned that when I feel guilty, I am living in the past. My past has come into my present, and I'm missing out on the wisdom and compassion that I could have taken from that moment from my past. I'm also covering up the flow of perfection, unconditional love and forgiveness that is available to me at all times.

Here are some special exercises you can use to forgive yourself and others, as well as ways to ask for forgiveness. I pray that you go through these exercises and release yourself from the past. Let it go. It's over. It's done. Be present *now*.

Asking Forgiveness for Something You Have Done

Most often, we need to forgive ourselves for things that we've done in the past.

Judgment, guilt, shame - these all come to the forefront when we can't forgive ourselves for something we've done in our past. If the experience means approaching another person for something you've done, and that doesn't feel quite right to you, you can still be forgiven all on your own. Forgiveness happens in consciousness. Since we are all one, the act of asking for forgiveness in a thoughtful, conscious way will shift you and the person involved - without his or her even knowing about your intentions.

The first step to forgiveness is to allow yourself to tell the story of what you have done one last time, to someone you trust, like a close friend or a counselor. Then, you let it go. This means not bringing the story up anymore, letting it truly stay in the past so it doesn't keep coming up in your present moment, defining who you are. Bringing up a memory over and over again only keeps it alive, and all of the guilty energy keeps coming right back to the forefront.

Then, create a private forgiveness ritual one evening, when the kids have gone to bed. Light a candle, brew some tea and sit comfortably, in the lotus position if possible, with some paper next to you. Close your eyes and center yourself, relaxing into your chair, letting go of the day, letting go of conversations and the to-do list – just let yourself relax.

Picture the person in your mind that you want to ask for forgiveness. Say what you need to say in your mind to him or her, and act as if the person is right there in front of you. If it feels good, open your eyes and write down what you want to say. Then, close your eyes and listen. Just be still and listen. *Is there any intuitive wisdom coming up for you?* If not, it is absolutely okay.

Next, send love. Remember that the person you are asking for forgiveness from was not there with you in that past experience by accident. There was a divine knowing happening for him or her too. Ask that person what he or she learned from the experience. See it from the other person's perspective. Let him or her respond to you after you ask for forgiveness. Watch that person say to you, "I forgive you." When you are done, say "goodbye" however it feels comfortable to you.

Most often, we also need to forgive ourselves for things that we've done in the past. So now, as the other person has left your consciousness, begin by saying to yourself, "I forgive myself now, for what I did. Repeat the following affirmations as you breathe and let in forgiveness:

I let go now, I relax into peace.

I am love. I move only from the now-moment.

I let my memories be in the past and I move up and on with the divine wisdom that was hidden inside.

To know better is to do better – I do better now.

I am free now of my past – I let it go.

I no longer judge myself with this memory. I let it be. I am whole perfect and complete right now.

Be with yourself for as long as you need to in order to set yourself free from this memory. Let yourself feel a sense of lightness. What you are doing is loving yourself enough that let old memories be what they are – *old* memories. You learned from them and can let them go. You are not defined by your past. You are only defined by how you are today.

Forgiving Someone for Hurting You

Forgiving another person allows you to release the memory and be free.

Many of us have someone in our pasts that we've been carrying with us in our minds. We might feel full of resentment because this person "deserves it". You might still be very angry about something that someone did to you and you can't let it go. But aren't you tired of carrying this memory with you? It's heavy, emotionally and physically, isn't it? It's only affecting *you* and *your* quality of life. If you feel ready to be present, and free from your past, you can forgive someone without even seeing that person, just as in the above exercise. This is my version of a meditation that I did with my own spiritual practitioner in the past.

Just as you did when you are seeking forgiveness for something you did to someone else in the past, share your story privately one final time to a trusted friend or counselor. Let that person know that you are telling this story for the very last time. Get it all out and make sure there is nothing left unsaid.

Then, one evening when the kids are in bed, create your own ritual to forgive the person who hurt you. Get into your meditation position, sitting comfortably in a chair with your feet on the floor, or on the ground in a lotus position. Have paper and pen next to you to record your thoughts afterwards. Breathe in and out slowly. Relax. Let go of your day.

Now bring to mind the person that you want to forgive. Remember that you are completely protected as you bring this person into your mind. No one can harm you. You are in charge of this guided exercise. Look closely at this person. Now, picture him gradually, slowly growing younger. See him as a high school student, and as a junior high student. See him as a 10 year-old, and as a five year-old. Take your time seeing him getting younger and younger. Now see him as a two year-old toddler, and then as a little, tiny baby lying there in front of you. Look at this sweet innocent baby lying there, kicking its feet and drooling as he squirms happily on the floor.

When you see the person as a baby, it reminds you that we were all born innocent and free. As soon as you are ready, looking closely at this little baby in front of you, offer your forgiveness. "I forgive you. You are free from my life. I am free from your life." Tell him that you learned what you needed to learn from the experience, and that he can let go of you as well. If you feel comfortable, feel free to pick the baby up and hold it.

You two were brought together for a bigger purpose than you can see, deeper than you might ever realize. Look into the baby's eyes, so small and open and innocent. Let him know that you are letting all attachments to him go now. You are releasing yourself from the hold of the past and the memory that has been weighing you down.

When you are ready, stand back and watch the baby grow back up into adulthood. Say goodbye to him. And when it feels right, open your eyes. Write down any thoughts that come to mind. Remember: forgiveness only needs to create changes in *your* mind. You are the one holding onto the resentment, after all. Forgiving another person allows you to release the memory and be free. Use these affirmations to support the release of the memory:

I release my past. It is over.

I let go. I am free. I release and let it all go!

I move on and allow for the now moment to be what guides me.

On-the-Spot Forgiveness

The more we accept each other's mistakes in life, the more we will accept our own mistakes.

Forgiveness is strongly connected to compassion. When you forgive yourself, you are allowing yourself to make a mistake. You are recognizing that we human beings are all learning as we go along through life. When you forgive someone else, you are making a space in your consciousness to be free. You are not allowing someone else's choice to affect your current life.

If I get cut off by another driver when I'm in my car, and feel angry about it, I say to myself, "I forgive myself for any time I've cut someone off in traffic and didn't realize it." When my two older children tease and fight with

117

A Mother's Manual for Self-Love

each other and I start to feel my blood boil I say, "I forgive myself for anytime I teased and fought with my siblings." If I'm at a birthday party with my kids and I hear two moms talking poorly about another mom, instead of judging them I say, "I forgive myself for any time I gossiped about someone."

This on-the-spot forgiveness brings compassion to the situation, making me a part of it instead of a victim, and I handle the particular situation in a much clearer way than I would have if I'd just reacted in anger. How much more compassionate this world will be when we can each hold the perspective that we are all one! We all make mistakes, we all raise our voices, and we all do things that we wish we hadn't. The more we accept each other's mistakes in life, the more we accept our own.

Forgiving ourselves in the moment allow us to have compassion for ourselves and others, and to move on with the gift of a bigger, more open heart. Here are some sample situations and affirmations for on-the spot forgiveness, and as you practice them every day, you'll find yourself growing lighter and freer in your spirit.

(*When a friend passes me by without saying hello*) I forgive myself for every time I was so much in my own head that I didn't realize who was around me.

(*When someone is endlessly trying to get me to believe in what he believes*) I forgive myself for anytime I thought I knew better for someone else.

(*When my child continually speaks in a whiney voice*) I forgive myself for every time I whined to my parents as a child, and when I whine now as an adult.

(*When I hear someone bad-mouthing someone else*) I forgive myself for anytime that I said something about a person that I would never say to her face.

(*When someone speaks to me rudely or abruptly on the phone*) I forgive myself for every time I've snapped at

A Mother's Manual for Self-Love

someone because I felt busy or overwhelmed by my to-do list.

(*When someone is not listening to me very well*) I forgive myself for all the times I let my mind wander instead of really listening to another person, or when I've made someone else feel insignificant because I wasn't listening wholeheartedly.

Releasing a Burden

You can be re-birthed into a new, more compassionate space and begin again.

Each of us can feel weighted down inside if we hold on to the memory of a mistake we've made, or when we follow an old pattern that isn't good for us. A friend of mine used to use her credit card to buy the kids all the holiday toys that they wanted, and then she punished herself mentally each time she received the monthly credit card bill. She got to feel punished and burdened by what she did in the past, month after month. For me, there is something here in her story about feeling unworthy, about feeling that she had to be punished for the way she was. Maybe she believed that she needed to hurt herself in this way. But, that pattern feels so heavy. It weighed her down every time she got that reminder of what she did.

No matter what your burden is, right now in this very moment you can choose to let the burden go. You can be re-birthed into a new, more compassionate space and begin again. Let's use my credit card example to demonstrate how we can let go of our past in any situation.

Pretend that you are the person who made the decision to charge too many gifts for her children. As part of the exercise, pretend that she is a dear, treasured friend of yours. You know she meant well when she bought all those gifts. You also know she feels awful about the debt. This is a friend that you feel honored to help. Now imagine that you are a new, completely burden-free person – light as a feather – who is also starting from scratch. You get to choose who you are from this point forward, living debt-free from this point forward. And, you choose to help out your beloved friend with her bills. You feel delighted to get to help her. You know she won't use her credit card anymore and that you can help her out each month. Now, let's ask you - as the amazing, new self that you are who chooses to help her friend out with her debt - some questions:

1. As the new *you*, what do you feel about yourself?

2. What do your friends value about you?

3. What are your favorite things about you?

4. How do you choose to be in relationship with money?

The whole point of this exercise is to allow you to let go of a decision that you made in the past. You are not your past. You can let go of those choices and create a new space for yourself. Embrace a more loving, healthy self that deserves a fresh, new start. When that credit card bill comes in the mail you can say,

"Oh, that old me, I'm so grateful I can help her out. I'm so grateful I don't use money anymore to make myself feel like I'm valued! I know that my friends and children and family love me for the gifts I give them in friendship, in listening, in using my sense of humor! I am enough just as I am –with no gifts in tow!"

Let go of your past. Forgive yourself now! You can use this exercise with any burden you are carrying. And every time it comes up for you, see yourself through kind eyes. And instead of groaning every time the credit card bill comes in the mail or your thoughts get pulled to a burden you are holding onto from your past, feel grateful that you can help a friend - *yourself* - with your old choices by being kind to yourself now.

Conversation with Your Future Self

What you are asking for is guidance that allows you to see the bigger picture.

I learned this exercise when I was working with my life coach, and it transformed my ability to witness my life from my own perspective. It also helped me to feel like I have skills for honoring the needs and wants of each of my children. This exercise asks you to look ahead and see yourself in the future, asking this older, wiser *you* for empowering guidance about something in the present. What you are asking for is guidance that allows you to see the bigger picture.

Start by sitting quietly wherever you are comfortable. Calm your mind until you feel peaceful and still. We will start with you, visualizing the person you will be 20 years from now. Imagine a house. Look closely at this house, noticing its color, that landscape around it, its size and what it is made of.

Now walk up to the house and knock on the door. When the door opens, it is you in 20 years. Look at the future you. What are you wearing? What do you look like? Are you smiling? Are you there with anyone? Greet yourself and allow your older version of you to love you and nurture you with a warm hug.

Next, walk into the house with your future self, where the two of you sit down together. Begin to ask your older version of yourself some questions, and pay attention to what comes up for you:

"Is there anything I can be doing right now that I'm not doing or that I'll wish I did?"

"I have this problem going on right now (describe it). Do you have any guidance about how to get through it?"

"What do you want me to know about my life right now?"

"Do you have any insights about my children for me?"

"What do you wish I had accomplished in my present life, something that I feel I have no time to do?"

Feel free to ask any other questions you have and listen to what this future you ahs to share. As you finish your conversation, thank your older version of yourself for her guidance and insight. Let her walk you to the door as you leave the house and return in your mind back to where you are right now. Go ahead and write down any insights you have received.

A Conversation with Your Grown-Up Child

Have you ever stewed over what decision to make for your child, like - would he want to take an extra science class, or will football at his age be too hard for him? We are always wondering what decision is best for our kids. Sometimes we can feel like we are *guessing* what to do, or like we are on our own in making a decision. Of course, we can go inside ourselves for intuitive guidance and we can also go deeper than that! We have the ability to connect with our child's own divine wisdom. We are all connected, so why not try tapping into your child's guidance to help you make a decision about his life?

Begin by getting quiet and comfortable. Breathe in and out slowly, relaxing in a chair. When you feel calm and peaceful and still, imagine a house. What do you see? Is there a yard? Is it a home in a suburb, or in the city? Look at the outside of the home – is it brick or siding? What color is it? What do the windows look like? As you notice these visual details, start walking up to the front door. When you get there, knock and wait until the door is opened. The door opens and there, standing in front of you, is your child! But he is an adult, the adult he will be. Notice how old he is. Picture him in detail. What is he wearing? How does his voice sound? How does he greet you?

Your grown-up child invites you into his home, and you both sit down. Picture the room you are in. Are you both sitting at a table? Are you sharing a living room couch? When you are ready, begin a conversation with your child. Ask him every question you can think of about this decision you're trying to make. For example:

"How are you doing now?"

"You are going through a particular problem at your young age now. How do you want me to handle it?"

"What do you need from me right now, as a young child?"

"As an adult, what do you wish we did as a family that we don't do now?"

"Is there anything I can change about how I mother you that will be more supportive of your growth?"

After you finish asking all of your questions, give your son a big hug and share all the gratitude with him you desire. Say good-bye and walk out of the house as he closes the door behind you. You know you can come back any time. Open your eyes as you bring yourself back to the present moment. Feel free to journal about the messages you received. You can do this exercise regularly, using one child a day or a week – whatever is convenient for you and your time.

Start a Worry Journal

This sounds a little counterproductive, doesn't it? Well, within the right parameters, journaling about your worries can be very useful. Grab a notebook and make four columns, each with its own title. Above the first column, write "What am I worried about?" For the second column, write, "What do I think is going to happen?" For the third, "What actually happened?" And the fourth column is "What action step can I take?"

Then, start writing down in column one and column two every worry and anxious thought that goes through your head, and what you fear the outcome will be. After a week or so, look back on these worries and see how many of them actually came true. Use the third column to note what really happened. Then, jot down in the fourth column what you can do to make yourself less vulnerable to that worry in the future.

The point of this exercise is for you to see for yourself that much of your worrying is actually misplaced energy that could be used to promote positive life changes instead.

You'll find that it feels good to see that your worry didn't really change the outcome of the situation, or help your life. It just made you stressed out, and probably stressed out the people around you too.

An important piece of advice: keep this worry journal for just a couple of weeks and then let it go. Focusing on worry can bring on more worry. This is only a short-term exercise to highlight how worry is neither productive nor necessary, and how choosing to trust in the flow of life brings peace and serenity.

Here are a few examples of a worry journal page:

What am I worried about?

1. There's a tornado warning.

2. It's the first day of school for my child.

3. I'm going to be hit by this recession.

What do I think is going to happen?

1. Tornado will hit house. Family gets hurt.

2. He'll get made fun of. He won't make any friends. He'll miss me. He won't fit in.

3. I'll lose my house. I'll lose my job. I'll end up homeless. How will I afford to raise the kids?

What actually happened?

1. No tornado, just a good thunderstorm. Drove husband crazy and scared the kids.

2. He came home from his first day and said he had fun! On the other hand, I didn't! I worried/stressed out and felt sick. I got other people to worry with me. I really made my child out to be a helpless victim.

3. I haven't lost my job, my home is fine. I got stressed out and wasn't focused at work. I felt depressed and worried – but nothing has happened! My kids and husband had to deal with my stress.

What action step can I take so that I don't worry about this anymore?

1. Learn about what steps to take if a tornado were to come. Practice meditation so I am prepared the next time there is a tornado warning. Have a routine ready, a plan that I can anchor myself in when a warning comes. Have an affirmation that reminds me of my worry journal page, so I'm not paralyzed by my worry.

2. Trust that my child is on his perfect path. Trust that he will find his way. Start my affirmations a week or so ahead of the start of school so that I am prepared to let him go to school and feel at peace about it. Prepare myself in advance with breathing meditations and calming thoughts. Take action – when I trust that my child will be okay, my child will trust in that knowledge too!

3. Arm myself with knowledge. Show up to work fully available. Practice meditation and connecting with my inner peace. Remember that the sun is always there - it's sometimes covered by clouds, but it is always there. Trust that I am safe and sound, no matter what happens in my life. Take action - become more aware of my spending, put money away, use coupons, shut off unnecessary lights/electricity, be more creative with free entertainment!

Beginning of Your Day Meditation

We are all spiritual beings, so we all have access to our inner guidance at any time.

As moms, our minds keep our thoughts running continuously all day long. From the minute we wake up, we start planning our day. Meditation is the special time you give yourself to clear your head from all of that constant chatter. You give yourself a true moment of peace. Picture your mind's chattering like a motor running. When you meditate, you turn the engine off and allow for it to rest. When we meditate, intuition is louder, and guidance is clearer. When our mind stops running its stories, we are calmer, more peaceful and available to hear whatever guidance we need. Knowing that there is wisdom inside of me about raising my children also allows me to see that I am never alone. It gives me confidence in my mothering, and most importantly, it gives me confidence in myself.

If you are new to meditation, it might sound difficult to do, or scary, or perhaps you worry that you don't have enough time. I promise you, none of that is true. We are all spiritual beings, so we all have access to our inner guidance at any time. And we all have time to meditate. A *conscious* breath, inhaling and exhaling, is meditation. You can even meditate for just 10 seconds – a pause to rein yourself in if you are feeling stressed out.

My goal for meditation is to meditate twice a day – once in the morning and once in the evening. I also connect with my inner place of peace with mini-meditations throughout the day. It isn't always perfect -and that is okay. I created a space in my bedroom to meditate in, a sort of altar, with a journal, some angel cards, some statues, mala beads, and some inspirational books. Here's a simple meditation for you to begin with:

Find a place in your home that feels comfortable to you. Maybe it's in a chair in the bedroom or on the floor of your living room. Maybe it's outside. You want your meditation place to be one that you feel peaceful in. Sit with your feet on the floor or in lotus position if you can.

Put your arms on the chair or on your knees – wherever it is are comfortable. Close your eyes.

Imagine that you have just shut down the motor in your mind. Your thoughts are off and unplugged. Breathe in and out, slowly, through your nose. Pay attention to the sensation of the air moving in and out through your nose. If a stray thought comes up, just notice it – don't judge it. Call it what it is – a thought. And let it go. Picture this thought as a bubble that floats away as soon as you realize its presence. Continue in this breathing space for 5 minutes for starters. Over time, you will feel more and more at ease as you practice, and the time you spend will expand.

Just being present to your senses is meditation. If you are available to the moment that is happening right now - you can see it, hear it, feel it - you are in meditation. How often are you present?

Mini-meditations throughout your day are wonderful. In any given moment as the day flows by, I close my eyes and breathe as I center myself back into that state of peace from my earlier morning meditation. I open my eyes. And that is it.

Ending Your Day Meditation

Evening meditation is a powerful way to let your day go as you prepare for sleep.

After taking care of the children and getting them to bed, all moms need some time for themselves to wind down and release themselves from the events of that day. Evening meditation is a powerful way to let your day go as you prepare for sleep.

Choose a place in your home that feels relaxing. It might be on your bed or on the patio - wherever you feel like you can unplug yourself from everything that took place that day. If you can sit in a lotus position, that's great. If not, just sit comfortably with your feet on the floor. (I also know how tired we can be at the end of the day, so if lying down on your bed feels like the most desirable option, please do so!)

Close your eyes. Breathe in and out slowly. As you breathe, go through your day in your mind. Is there anything left over that feels heavy on your heart? Is there anything that you wish you'd handled differently? Ask for the lesson in it – see if you can find some gift in any situation that you wish played out differently.

After you receive the lesson, replay the day's scenario in your head so that this time it happens the way that you wish it had. Then, let it go. Give it up and release it. This allows you to go to sleep without anything weighing heavily on your heart.

Next, go through the day's events that you are grateful for. Breathe in and out as you express your gratitude.

As I end this meditation, I close by relaxing each body part, starting with my toes and moving up through to the top of my head. Every part of me relaxes, and my sleep is easy and peaceful.

Preparation for Family Changes

The more we are prepared in advance, the better we will react when we are with our children during changes in the family routine.

I don't know about you, but when my child starts something new, I tend to feel a bit stressed about it. I have trigger points, like when my child starts school and I'm wondering whether he'll like his teacher or if he'll make friends. When school is out for the summer, the first week or so of that transition can be challenging too. After all, the kids are used to being at school and I am used to my own routine. Suddenly, all routines change! Families face countless other changes as well that can shift the family dynamic.

I have developed some "preparation work" that really helps me to get ready for any big changes that I know about ahead of time. Preparing ourselves as the moms also helps the energy in our family and with our kids. It helps us feel more confident and sure of ourselves, and of our children. My first example of this preparation practice will be for when your child starts school, maybe even for the first time.

About one month before the big transition, start with affirmations for yourself. This gets you ready for anything that might come up in the week or two before your child starts school. You'll feel prepared when you go to registrations or open houses. By the time school begins, you'll be so "affirmed-up" that you'll breeze through the first week. Sure, you might still feel some jitters, and I want to honor those as well.

Here are some affirmations that I have used which will support your personal health and offer comfort when the time comes to send your child off to school. (You can actually use these affirmations for absolutely anything that is coming up in your family life that is different from your normal routine.)

My child is on his perfect path.

I am supportive of my child's schooling and I know that he will have his perfect experience.

I count on intuition to inform me of anything I need to know.

If my child is nervous, I allow for my confidence and security to show through for him.

My child draws balanced, loving friends to him that support his growth.

I imagine my child as an adult and see him successful and happy. I know he is well.

I trust in the process of my child's life. I trust that I am the perfect mother to guide him the way he needs to be guided.

Another big change in family life is when summer vacation begins. It can be such a fun and wonderful and challenging time – all at the same time! Here are some affirmations to support you as you prepare for summer break.

I am prepared and ready to be a balanced, joyful mother.

I enjoy the change in routine and relax into the new shift.

I look for intuitive guidance to lead my way all of the time.

I am never alone – I am always co-creating with spirit.

I love myself and accept myself for how I show up.

I love my children and I look forward to our growth

I remain light and in control so we can all have fun

I loosen up with rules so that summer can bring relief

All of my responsibilities are cared for with ease and grace

I take care of myself physically and mentally so I am prepared for anything that comes up.

My kids are kids and perfection is in the imperfection

I call forth my deep love to be palpable during difficult times

I look forward to the joy and love and bonding we get to have!

The more we are prepared in advance, the better we will react when we are with our children during changes in the family routine. And, the more we believe – without a doubt - that we are being led by our intuition, and our children are on their perfect paths, the less worry we have, and the more we can enjoy this sacred job of being mothers!

Mother's Self Love Meditation

It's so important to realize that our children will not treat themselves the way that we treat them, they will treat themselves the way we treat ourselves.

Sit somewhere comfortable for you - in a chair, on the floor, or on your bed – with your legs crossed in a lotus position if you can. Be comfortable! Have a notebook or piece of paper and pen nearby. Rest your hands on your knees, palms facing upwards. Close your eyes. Breathe in and out slowly and thought-fully. (By "thought-fully" I mean bringing your awareness to this now-present moment.) Pay attention to each breath going in and out through your nose.

As you begin to still your mind, bring your thoughts to a time when you were totally and completely in your love. It could be a feeling that came over you when you heard your child's first laugh, or when you first fell in love with your spouse - there is no right or wrong here. Feel it. Where did you feel that memory in your body? How did you feel? Immerse yourself in *that* feeling of love, as if it's happening right now. Sit in this feeling for a few moments. Now, bring your attention to your heart space. Picture your heart with glowing energy all around it, a green-colored energy that is expanding outward, just through your awareness of it.

Now picture your child's heart. See the warm, green energy expanding all around it. See this heart energy in you connecting with the heart energy around your child's heart. It's warm and beautiful. It's like a cord connecting the two of you together. Now, through this connection within your heart space, ask yourself, "What things do I want for my child's life?"

Some ideas to get you started are:

You are loved.

I want you to see your greatness.

I want you to accept yourself for who you are.

I want you to love who you are.

I want you to have healthy positive friendships.

I want you to love what you do.

I want you to be happy.

When you have completed your list of desires for your child, close your eyes again and center inward. If you have other children, go ahead and connect with them, one at a time and ask the same questions. When you complete this meditation for each child, breathe in and out a few times until you feel your mind calm and peaceful. Then ask yourself this question:

How am I embodying these desires for my children in my own life?

Journal a bit on what comes up for you. When you are ready, you can close your eyes again, centering back into the peace. Visualize that beautiful, warm green energy around your heart space. See it vibrantly expanding throughout your whole body. Send this loving energy to your legs, to your arms, to your voice box, to your eyes. Know that you have access to this loving energy at all times.

You can open your eyes when you are ready.

Moms - it's so important to realize that children will not treat themselves the way that we treat them, they will treat themselves the way we treat ourselves. When I did this exercise I found that the things I wanted to give my children were things I wasn't giving myself. I was going to be a very poor teacher until I realized this and changed my thinking. I deserve everything that I want for my children. Be a teacher that walks the walk. Love yourself, experience your joy, and know that your joy is just as important as your child's joy!

Connecting to Your Inner Child Meditation

Your inner, magical child is with you.

This meditation, which brings me so much comfort, helps me to realize that I am not just the one-dimensional person I sometimes feel like I am today. I have access to myself at all of my ages, even ages I haven't yet reached! When I connect to my inner child – the ME that used to fantasize about being the very age I am now - I want to affirm and honor the dreams she once had for me. I owe her more of my attention. I also owe my children a taste of "me" as I was a child.

Find a quiet place, a place in your home that fills you with calm energy. Create a sacred place for yourself with a candle or incense or fresh flowers. Sit comfortably with your feet on the ground, or in lotus position. Put your hands on the arms of the chair or on your knees – wherever you feel the most comfortable. Close your eyes.

Breathe in and out, slowly, picturing your breath going in and out of your nose. See the air moving slowly and effortlessly in and out, in and out. Center yourself, letting go of anything that happened earlier in the day, or anything to come later in your day. Notice the sounds and smells around you. Allow your thoughts to slowly disappear. Quiet your mind. Breathe.

Now, bring to mind a memory from your childhood that seemed magical. Did you play house or pretend like you had your own babies? Did you daydream then about what it would be like to be an adult? Did you feel like you had the world in your hands? Was it summertime, when you could play outside all day without a care in the world?

Think about yourself as that child. See her. Connect with her innocence, her carefree imagination, her playful spirit. Go into that memory. See yourself in an outfit you used to love to wear – maybe it was extra-comfortable, or maybe you just remember it from pictures. Did you wear pigtails, or did you have short hair, or curly hair? Look at the child that is *you*.

That little child is still inside of you. She exists right now. She has your eyes and your smile. And she wants to play! You and she are the same person. You have her crazy imagination and playful spirit right inside of you. Connect with her. See her and ask her what she thinks about your life right now? Is it what she pictured? What wisdom does she have for you? Ask her. She *is* you, so she has answers for you. How does this inner child want to show up in your life right now? What does she want to say to you?

When you feel ready, open your eyes. Write down any messages you received from your inner child. And, bring your inner child into your days as you are with your kids. Let her be proud of you. Let her know that she is heard, and that she can be joyful knowing she is still alive in you. Remember - your inner, magical child is always with you.

While You Work Meditation

Being totally present – whatever you're doing - is a form of meditation.

During your day, wherever you are – whether at the office or at home taking care of your family - you can practice meditation. Meditation is about being totally available to the moment you are in, right now. The more you practice being totally present, the more available you are to inner guidance and wisdom that is always there to serve you.

When I find myself sitting in front of a big pile of laundry, I begin the process of meditation in gratitude. I say how thankful I am to have a washer and dryer. I say how thankful I am to have clothes to fold. I say how happy I am to have children. Then, I fold the clothes very mindfully. I pay full attention to the creases I press, and to the way the clothes feel in my hands. I focus on getting the clothes into the right piles. I am totally present with the task at hand. Being totally present – whatever you're doing - is a form of meditation.

When you are driving to the office, feel the car seat underneath you and the steering wheel in your hands. Pay attention to the cars and other people around you...the smells, the sights, the sounds. Feel gratitude as you enter your place of work. With a smile, notice every person that walks by you. Keep that gratitude going for your co-workers, for the job you have, for your family, and for your abundance. Do your sacred work mindfully, as this job is a way that you are taking care of yourself and the needs of your family.

When you are home washing the dishes, pay attention to the temperature of the water, the soap on your hands, the dishes piled in the sink. Again, begin in gratitude, "How grateful I am for having water that comes out of a faucet so effortlessly, to have dishes to clean, to have food to eat, to have a family to feed." Then do your sacred work of cleaning up the kitchen – or, more sacredly put - *taking care of yourself and the needs of your family.*

I hope that this Working Meditation helps you to find your daily commitments a little more enjoyable and relaxing. As you practice this *mind-full* work, you will find yourself more able to concentrate easily, and focus with less effort. This will also help create an opening for intuition to be more available to you. You will also be creating a sacred space for the every day jobs that you have to do. Enjoy!

Unconditional Love Meditation

You are love, my dear moms. You deserve to know it and believe it about yourself!

When we are reacting to something happening in our lives, we can forget about being unconditionally loving. This mantra meditation brings awareness to the fact that we ARE unconditional love. That there is no limit to the amount of love we have to give, and that we have the ability to be compassionate and allowing at all times.

This meditation can be done while you are on the move, or while you sit in a comfortable chair or on the floor in a lotus position. I find it to be powerful while I am getting ready in the morning, helping me remember that I have the ability to exude unconditional at all times. If you are sitting, rest your hands on your knees with your palms open and facing upwards. Close your eyes.

Breathe slowly and fully in and out. When you feel relaxed and centered, begin to picture different parts of your body and see the unconditional love to be found in each part. Only move to the next body part when you really feel that love. Soak up this unconditional love for yourself. Internalize these words – really feel them! If you are busy getting ready in the morning, you can still keep your thoughts focused on the words.

Here is the pattern that I follow:

My legs move me in unconditional love. (*Deep inhale and exhale.*)

My feet hold me in unconditional love. (*Deep inhale and exhale.*)

My arms are used for unconditional love. (*Deep inhale and exhale.*)

My hands hold and touch with unconditional love. (*Deep inhale and exhale.*)

My heart is filled with unconditional love. (*Deep inhale and then exhale.*)

My stomach is unconditionally loving as it digests my food and nurtures my body. (*Deep inhale and exhale*)

The essence of my voice box expresses unconditional love. (*Deep inhale and then exhale.*)

My words come from unconditional love. (*Deep inhale and then exhale.*)

My eyes see with unconditional love. (*Deep inhale and then exhale.*)

My ears hear with unconditional love. (*Deep inhale and then exhale.*)

My brain processes knowledge and conversations with unconditional love. (*Deep inhale and exhale*)

My facial expressions exude unconditional love at all times. (*Deep inhale and then exhale.*)

I am unconditional love. (*Deep inhale and then exhale.*)

Moms, it feels so good to know that every aspect of you is part of this unconditional love. Nothing is left out. The voice box mantra is the one that I feel the deepest. I challenge you to find the one that resonates the most with you, and keep it alive in your mind throughout your day. You are love, my dear moms. You deserve to know it and believe it about yourself! The more you believe it about yourself, the more you will show it to others.

Changing a Behavior

When I feel I've been pushed to my limit, I get to what I would call "losing it". I react unconsciously, because it truly feels like I'm teetering at the edge of my universe. For me, this comes out as either yelling or shutting down. When I give this scenario a visual image, it looks like a circle, where my life is inside the circle but the experience I'm having right now is one step outside the circle. I know that I have the opportunity in that very sacred moment to expand my circle of life, to include this experience. But, how do I do this?

The answer I've learned: Do whatever would be the complete opposite reaction. The first time I did this, I broke out into what seemed like crazy, hysterical laughter. My kids thought I was nuts! What the laughter did though, was to break me out of the pattern of believing that the only way to react in this situation is to yell. When the crazy laughter stopped, I could see things differently. Light had been shed on the situation and I didn't just *react*. I saw the situation from a new perspective.

Other wonderful ways to shake yourself out of your anger or shame or resentment are to dance, or to hug your child, or to say, "I love you" to yourself, out loud! You could also run in circles, start singing, or do jumping jacks. Anything that pulls you out of your familiar reactive pattern and into a new state of consciousness will work. As you practice this more and more, you will also notice that that edge of the circle you were teetering on is no longer where it used to be. The circle has gotten bigger and you are allowing more experiences in your life.

Have fun with this! Your inner child will be ecstatic!

Affirmations

As my kids have gotten older I find that I might linger in worrying thoughts about them. I started a habit a while ago that I do most mornings for them, so I can stay in the trust that they are well. I state affirmations like:

I know that my child is whole, perfect and complete. I ask that she sees people and situations with kind eyes and she speaks from her deeper voice. I ask that she rise above chaos. I trust that she makes good choices and she believes deeply in herself today. I claim she is a good friend and friends are good to her. I ask that she be ignorant to judgment and be a crusader of inclusion. I ask that a veil of safety be placed around her today from illness and or injury. I trust that no matter what she comes home with, it's exactly where she is supposed to be and I trust her growth- whatever it looks like. I trust that I know how to respond to any situation that comes my way. I'm grateful to know this for her today. And so it is!

Prayer for Your Kids (feel free to use other terms such as love, god, universe, life, etc...)

I lie in bed and now I pray - I'm so thankful for this day.

God, show me my wisdom to see me through the things that feel bad or scary or new.

I send love light and blessings to all my friends and family and to those I have troubles with -

God please help me.

I pray for those who are sick or who have lost their homes knowing there is love in their hearts and they are never alone.

I am grateful so grateful for all that I am - please help me be the best that I can. And so it is.

Thank you!

I want to thank so many people for helping me on this journey of being a mom and writing this book. Thank you to Bodhi Spiritual Center for being my safe space to fall. Thank you to Sara Connell for being a light in the dark, Mark Anthony Lord for being my teacher, Chris Marr, Jeannie Jordan, Cherie Jones, Maureen O'Malley, Kris Nielsen, The infinite eight: Darrell Jones, Linda Michaels, Joan Coletto, Kate Miller, Tonya Melendez, Marguerite LaLonde, Kim Revere...Patrick Ziegler, Emilio and Julie Salvi for walking my ready to deliver self to the hospital from work almost 14 years ago, and for watching the other kids when the others were born, Terry Pfister, Kemery Bloom Derby, Angela Quintieri, my Mom Support Group (you know who you are!), my Mom and Dad, my Mother-in-law, Annette Schrag, Bill Soucie, Danielle Norberg, Laura Soucie, Karen Soucie, Beth Schrag, and all of my in-laws and all of my nieces and nephews, all of my family, my unconditionally supportive husband, Brian, my beautiful children, Cooper, Sophie and Violet. I'd like to thank all of the moms out there that I've been privileged to know even if for a moment. I am so grateful for this journey.

Made in the USA
Lexington, KY
24 January 2017